Electronic Evidence

Alan M. Gahtan

CARSWELL
Thomson Professional Publishing

Canadian Cataloguing in Publication Data

Gahtan, Alan M.
  Electronic evidence

Includes index.
ISBN 0-459-27070-2

1. Evidence, Documentary — Canada. 2. Evidence, Documentary — United States. 3. Computer files — Law and legislation — Canada. 4. Computer files — Law and legislation — United States. I. Title.

KE8457.G33 1999   347.71'064   C99-931632-X
KF8947.G33 1999

CARSWELL
Thomson Professional Publishing

One Corporate Plaza, 2075 Kennedy Road, Scarborough, Ontario M1T 3V4
Customer Service:
Toronto: 1-416-609-3800
Elsewhere in Canada/U.S. 1-800-387-5164
Fax 1-416-298-5094

Foreword

... electronic discovery in legal cases has become a mini-industry with the discovery process itself having increasing impact on the outcome of litigation.[1]

The first part of this publication is designed to assist lawyers, judges and investigators in gaining a better understanding of the various types of electronic evidence that may exist and to provide guidance on how to go about locating such evidence. Chapter 6 sets out defensive strategies that can be used to mitigate the potential risks and costs associated with having to respond to a request for electronic discovery. The objective is to assist potential litigants (both plaintiff and defendant) in identifying and correcting any weaknesses in their systems and procedures. The last part of this publication presents a multi-jurisdictional overview of some of the legal issues related to the preservation, disclosure and use of electronic evidence in judicial proceedings.

Now for the disclaimer: there are differences in the law between different jurisdictions and the law in this area is still evolving. If you are involved in a case where the use of electronic evidence is an issue then a more comprehensive review of the law in your particular jurisdiction will be required. It also goes without saying that this publication is not a substitute for legal advice from a lawyer who has researched the applicable areas of the law and can apply such knowledge to your particular circumstances. Also, the technology is undergoing rapid change. While this publication provides a good starting point, up-to-date and comprehensive assistance from a knowledgeable professional should be obtained by lawyers, their clients or government investigators who become involved in a matter with significant electronic media discovery implications.

I wish to acknowledge the assistance of Judy Chun who assisted with some of the research and an early draft of chapter 9. I also wish to acknowledge the following individuals who provided me with comments and feedback on various portions of the book: Robyn M. Bell, Carole L. Hunt and Robert W. Staley of Bennett Jones, Master Julian Polika, Case Management Master of the Ontario Court, and Timothy J.D. Pinos of Cassels Brock and Blackwell.

---

1 Geanne Rosenberg, "Electronic Discovery Proves Effective Legal Weapon" *The New York Times* (31 March 1997).

Table of Contents

Table of Cases

(The cases are referenced to section numbers)

1

Introduction to
Electronic Evidence

1.1 THE IMPORTANCE OF ELECTRONIC EVIDENCE

Of interest to a plaintiff, a company's database may contain an earlier and safer
design of a product that is the subject of a product liability suit; an earlier draft
of a sensitive document to prove intent in a fraud claim; altered spreadsheets
in an investor fraud case; company strategies to eliminate competitors in an
antitrust case; employment records in a discrimination case; memoranda evi-
dencing willful infringement in a patent case; and, of course, financial records
useful in just about any case.[1]

Computer technology has revolutionized the way we deal with information and the
way we run our businesses. Increasingly, important business information is being
created, stored and communicated electronically. Many types of information that
can play a useful role in litigation or criminal prosecutions are no longer printed
on paper and stored in paper files but rather are stored in a computer system or in
computer-readable form. As companies and individuals have increased their reliance on their computer systems, lawyers and investigators have begun to realize
the valuable electronic treasures that are now being kept in these systems and have
started aggressively to target electronic data for discovery and production in all
types of cases.[2] The discoverability of these electronic files is referred to as
"Electronic Media Discovery" or EMD.

---

1 Pooley & Shaw, "The Emerging Law of Computer Networks—Finding Out What's
  There: Technical and Legal Aspects of Discovery" (1996), online: <http://www.fr.
  com/pubs/paper21.html>.
2 One large multinational company, Dupont, saw the proportion of discovery requests for
  production which explicitly referred to electronic evidence or e-mail jump from 2% to
  30% in less than 5 years (ending in 1999).

Electronic evidence has been used for numerous purposes in recent cases including:

- to substantiate allegations of sexual harassment;[3]
- to prove theft of trade secrets by an employee[4] or others;[5]
- to validate copyright infringement[6] or verify the improper use of licensed software;[7]
- to obtain data to determine an individual's assets;
- to find evidence of fraudulent or criminal activity;
- to substantiate a wrongful termination of employment;[8]
- to provide evidence of insider trading;[9]
- to establish a relationship between a murder victim and the person accused of her murder; and

---

3 See *Knox v. State of Ind.*, 93 F.3d 1327 (7th Cir. (Ind.), 1996), where key evidence in a sexual harassment suit was e-mail messages in which a supervisor repeatedly asked for sex. See also *Harley v. McCoach*, 928 F. Supp. 533 (E.D.Pa., 1996).

4 For instance, see *People v. Eubanks and Wang*, Nos. C.R. 6748 (Ca. Supr. Ct.), a criminal trade secrets prosecution against a former Borland Vice President. One of the most frequent forms of misappropriation involves sales employees who take customer lists, pricing and information and marketing data (projections, plans and histories). Tracing data theft back to employees has allowed some companies to obtain crucial evidence in their efforts to restrain use of such data.

5 *First Technology Safety Systems, Inc. v. Depinet*, 11 F.3d 641 (6th Cir. (Ohio), 1993).

6 In software-related copyright infringement cases, access to the source code may be helpful in demonstrating that unauthorized access or copying had occurred. For instance, see *Prism Hospital Software Inc. v. Hospital Medical Records Institute*, 18 B.L.R. (2d) 1, 97 B.C.L.R. (2d) 201, [1994] 10 W.W.R. 305, 57 C.P.R. (3d) 129 (B.C. S.C.).

7 See *Lauren Corp. v. Century Geophysical Corp.*, 953 P.2d 200 (Colo.App., 1998).

8 For instance, in *Kelley v. Airborne Freight Corp.*, 140 F.3d 335 (1st Cir. (Mass.), 1998), *certiorari* denied by *Airborne Freight Corp. v. Kelley*, 119 S.Ct. 341 (U.S., 1998) the US Court of Appeal upheld a judgment awarding over US $ 4.3 million to an Airborne Express employee who alleged that he was wrongfully terminated based on age discrimination. At trial, Kelley had introduced e-mail messages exchanged between the company's corporate officers and his supervisors which demonstrated that the reasons given by Airborne for his termination were a pretext. See also M.R. Overly, "Effective Discovery of Electronic Evidence" *Orange Country Lawyer Magazine* (January 1997), online: <http://www.forensics.com/resources/discov.htm>, where the author describes an age discrimination case that was settled for $250,000 following the discovery of a salvaged e-mail message from the company's president to the head of the personnel department that contained discriminatory language and ordered the employee's termination.

9 See *Smith v. SEC*, 129 F.3d 356 (6th Cir. (Tenn.), 1997) at 359, where a voicemail message introduced as evidence included the following admission of wrongdoing: "I sold all my stock off on Friday, and I'm going to short the stock because I know it's going to go down a couple of points here in the next week, as soon as Lou releases the information about next year's earnings."

- to provide evidence of death threats sent by e-mail.[10]

(a) Plaintiffs' Lawyers

> For an attorney in modern litigation to ignore intangible, electronic data is to risk losing otherwise winnable cases; to risk exposing clients to expensive and otherwise avoidable judgments; to risk the imposition of sanctions for failure to produce, or for destruction of available files.[11]

Experienced litigators know that the outcome of a case is often determined during the discovery process. Plaintiffs' lawyers have, therefore, been increasingly targeting electronic evidence for a number of reasons:[12]

- Requests for discovery of electronic evidence can be used as a negotiating tool.[13] Information technologies, including e-mail, have led to the unprecedented proliferation and retention of large quantities of information. In the event of litigation, this can impose an extraordinary discovery burden on the possessor.[14] The increased use of messaging systems supporting the use of

---

10 See *U.S. v. Machado* (Feb. 12 1998), which involved the defendant sending racist death threats to Asian students attending the University of California, Irvine.

11 *Supra*, at note 1.

12 Of course, lawyers representing defendants may also wish to seek electronic evidence in the possession of plaintiffs.

13 Lawyers representing plaintiffs know that it can be very expensive for most unprepared large defendant organizations to preserve, search and quickly produce electronic evidence. The difficulty or cost of finding such data may not be excusable by a court, as reasons for not being able to produce relevant evidence. The discovery process is such a fundamental component of our justice system and any organization choosing to implement a complex computer system could design it in a way that more readily facilitates access to the information for discovery purposes. Even where electronic discovery is reciprocal, a plaintiff, who may be a smaller company or an individual, typically has significantly fewer electronic sources of data. In contrast, larger organizations bear disproportionate risks and burdens in having to comply with requests for electronic discovery. The threat of electronic discovery may, therefore, prompt a large party to settle.

In some cases, a review of electronic files by parties results in the parties realizing that their files actually contain information that they never knew existed or would prefer to keep under wraps. Consequently, such a party may be more open to negotiation and settlement of the matter, in order to avoid disclosure as required by the discovery process.

14 J. Novack, "Control/Alt/Discovery" *Forbes* (13 January 1997), quotes John Jessen, president of Electronic Evidence Discovery, as having a corporate client under court order to search 50,000 tapes, a process that was estimated to cost more than US $1 million.

multimedia will significantly increase the costs involved with retrieving and reviewing such messages.

- Access to incriminating evidence that the other party did not know existed[15] or thought was deleted[16] or not saved.[17]
- A growing proportion of information stored inside a computer system is never printed on paper.[18] For instance, aircraft maintenance manuals and maintenance records are often available in electronic form only.
- Electronic evidence may provide access to informal comments sent through an e-mail system that would not have been otherwise committed to writing in a formal document.[19]
- Even where paper printouts of documents or agreements are available, older draft versions may only be available in electronic form.[20]
- It may be possible to obtain electronic copies of paper-based documents[21] that were altered,[22] destroyed[23] or hidden.

---

15   Many types of computer software create usage logs or capture various types of information in electronic form without the knowledge of the user. Some companies may not even be aware that their computer software has captured such information in electronic form.

16   For instance, many e-mail users may incorrectly believe that deleting a particular e-mail message will also delete all other copies of that message.

17   Many organizations have well developed document retention programs for paper-based documents but less developed, if any, retention programs for electronic data or electronic versions of the paper documents. Backups are often performed of the entire computer system and a copy of all electronic information is captured to a backup tape.

18   Sometimes letters or memos are written or dictated but not printed and sent. Such documents do not leave the familiar paper trail that lawyers are accustomed to following during discovery questioning. It has been estimated that as much as 35% of electronic data does not make it into printed form. "What About 'Deleted' Files Still Subject to Discovery?" *The New Jersey Lawyer* (6 May 1996). See also, Jessen & Shear, "The Impact of Electronic Data Discovery on the Corporation" (National Conference of American Corporate Counsel Association, May 1994).

19   Electronic mail (e-mail) has become an important communication vehicle in many commercial enterprises. Its informal nature can lead to many things being said in an e-mail message that would not have otherwise been committed to writing in a more formal memo.

20   Older versions of documents and designs can track the evolution of a document and can be very revealing of decisions made during a design process. For instance, in a product liability case, older drafts may provide evidence that a company was aware of a design defect. Older drafts may also provide a better insight into the other party's intentions than a final draft that was edited for political correctness and legal considerations. These older copies may be retained on the computer system or may need to be restored from backup tapes.

21   For instance, schedules and to-do lists are increasingly being maintained in electronic form.

22   In other words, where a printed copy may have been altered or falsified, it may still be possible to uncover an original unaltered version that was stored in electronic form.

23   Many office workers are very bad at deleting electronic copies of documents and e-mail messages. Unlike paper-based documents that can be seen piling up on their desks by their supervisors, or overflowing the physical space limitations of an office file room,

- Electronic versions of documents or records may contain additional information.[24] Hidden codes or system information may be present in the electronic copy and may be used to detect tampering (such as changing the date of a document)[25] or provide information concerning the creation and distribution of a document.
- Electronic evidence can be more persuasive[26] than paper documents. An audio or multimedia message, obtained from an electronic messaging system supporting such capabilities, can be especially compelling.

(b) Prosecutors and Government Investigators

Computer systems, generally, and electronic evidence, in particular, have attracted the attention of government investigators. Many law enforcement agencies have recruited computer evidence specialists or have trained existing personnel.

Numerous statutory provisions empower government officials to enter, inspect, and make copies of records that must be maintained pursuant to various statutes and

---

electronic documents are not so visible. Many users would rather archive electronic information on a disk, and shove it in a drawer in case it is required again, than try to organize and delete material that is no longer necessary.

24 At least one court has recognized that the electronic version of a document may contain additional information that is not present when the document is viewed on the screen or printed out. In *Armstrong v. Executive Office of the President*, 810 F.Supp. 335 (D.D.C., 1993), decision affirmed and remanded by *Armstrong v. Executive Office of the President, Office of Admin.*, 1 F.3d 1274 (D.C.Cir., 1993), the Court of Appeal of the District of Columbia concluded that the electronic version of e-mail records contained additional information, such as transmission and reception dates, a detailed listing of recipients, linkages between messages sent and received, and other information that is not present in printed copies. It was insufficient for the government to preserve only the paper printouts of such messages. See also *Public Citizen v. Carlin*, 2 F.Supp. 2d 1 (D.D.C., 1997), which addressed the validity of a regulation that governed the disposal of electronic records created by agencies of the US federal government. The regulation, General Records Schedule 20 (GRS 20), permitted the destruction of electronic versions of word processing files and e-mail messages, once these records were backed up to an electronic, paper or microfilm based record keeping system. The court acknowledged that the electronic versions may not be identical to their paper counterparts and are unique and distinct from the printed versions of the same records. Consequently, the court found the destruction guidelines in GRS 20 were invalid under the *Federal Records Act* and the *Records Disposal Act*.

25 If the date a document was created is at issue, it may be useful to check the backup tape sets made during that period to see if a copy was backed up before the date it was alleged to have been created.

26 Some forms of electronic evidence, such as e-mail, are being used increasingly by a growing segment of our society. Many jurors, familiar with the use of e-mail in their own workplace, may give it increased weight as reflecting the author's more truthful and frank belief about a subject.

regulations.[27] The primary purpose of these provisions is to enable the government to determine whether a company is complying with the record keeping and other requirements contained in the statute that imposes them. Many businesses are increasingly storing the required records in electronic form. Government investigators will likely begin to focus their attention on the electronic form of these records and the computer systems that house them.

The government also has access to records for investigatory purposes. Several statutes, such as human rights codes, *Competition Act*, *Criminal Code* and tax acts give government officials the right to enter a business establishment and inspect or seize records. For example, under the *Competition Act*, peace officers with, or in exigent circumstances without, a search warrant, may enter the premises, examine records, and copy or seize them.[28] They may use the computer system on the premises to search data and produce printouts, which they may then seize for examination or copying.[29] Similar provisions are contained in various US legislation.

Computer data, particularly information thought to have been deleted, may be crucial to criminal prosecutors and police investigators. In *Com. v. Copenhefer*,[30] the defendant was convicted of first-degree murder based, in part, on evidence obtained from his computer's hard disk. The defendant had drafted and stored copies of a ransom note and other information detailing his kidnapping scheme. An FBI expert was able to retrieve copies of these documents that the defendant had mistakenly believed had been successfully deleted.

(c) Defendants' Lawyers

Lawyers representing parties with large amounts of electronic data need to understand that their clients' data will be targeted for such discovery and need to advise their clients on how to prepare. Defensive strategies that should be implemented prior to litigation include a proper document retention program, periodic purging of magnetic media and the implementation of a document management system. Once litigation has commenced, defendants need to be advised on how to preserve relevant electronic evidence adequately, in order to avoid possible sanctions or a negative inference at trial.

---

27 A 1993 report by the Ontario Law Reform Commission found that an authority to enter premises without a warrant was granted to government officials in 223 public Acts, 61 private Acts, 86 regulations and numerous by-laws—Ontario Law Reform Commission, *Report on Powers of Entry* (1983), at 8.

28 *Competition Act*, R.S.C. 1985 (2nd Supp.), c. 19, ss. 5(5), (7), (8).

29 S. 16(1).

30 587 A.2d 1353 (Pa. 1991), reargument denied (1991), denial of post-conviction relief affirmed by 719 A.2d 242 (P.A. 1998), reargument denied (1998).

1.2 WHY ELECTRONIC EVIDENCE IS DIFFERENT

Electronic data has several characteristics that differentiate them from more traditional paper evidence. A better understanding of the way electronic information is created, stored, maintained and destroyed in an organization is important so that appropriate steps can be taken in the early phases of an action to ensure that all sources of relevant electronic evidence can be properly preserved.

The most important characteristic of an electronic version of a document is that it may not be identical to the printed copy. Significant hidden information may only be visible during an examination of the electronic version. As a result, possession of the electronic copy of a document may yield more information than a supposedly complete printout of the same document.

Computers also routinely save information in locations, such as log files and document headers, that are not generally accessible to users. Many users are unaware of the many types of information that may be tracked and saved by computer systems without their knowledge.

Electronic data can also be stored very compactly. This can make it easier to move or lose electronic data as compared with paper-based evidence. Hiding a $3\frac{1}{2}$-inch diskette is easier than a filing room full of files. It is also significantly less time consuming and visible to destroy such a small diskette than to shred hundreds of pages in the file or photocopying room.

Electronic data is more vulnerable than paper-based documents. Electronic data can be more easily altered or forged as compared with information contained on paper or microfilm.[31] With proper technical knowledge, such alteration of electronic data may also be easier to cover up.

A review of a paper document is simply a matter of reading. An electronic document, on the other hand, may have been stored in any one of hundreds of different formats. In many cases, such documents can only be displayed in intelligible form when viewed through the software program used to create them. Even then, useful information may be hidden in the document and not easily accessible.

---

31 In one case, a former employee of Oracle, Adelyn Lee, sued the company for wrongful termination claiming that she had been fired by the company's chairman after she had broken off an affair with him. The suit was settled out of court for $100,000. It was later discovered that the incriminating e-mail she had offered as proof did not actually originate from the executive but rather had been forged by the employee. See M. Overley, "Finding the Needle in the Haystack: Discovering Electronic Evidence" *ILPN* (17 February 1997).

Once created, electronic data may be difficult to destroy. The computer staff, who are generally the ones in control of the electronic data, are usually averse to destroying it.[32]

Another differentiating characteristic of electronic data is its potential to proliferate. Photocopiers may have facilitated the copying of paper documents, but making and distributing electronic copies is even easier. Electronic documents tend to be stored in more locations and typically distributed to a wider audience than paper documents.[33] While individual electronic copies of documents may be easy to delete, the task of finding and erasing all copies and traces of a document can be much more challenging.

One computer forensic expert recited a case where her firm was called in to investigate suspicion that two employees had been setting up their own business with the client's product. The two employees had been careful to encrypt their e-mail messages. However, evidence was eventually found in the form of a deleted, but still recoverable, file containing a *PowerPoint* presentation that had been created for launching their new company.[34]

In the case of paper-based evidence, one person, acting alone, could usually review the available evidence and easily destroy or alter copies of incriminating material. Things have become more difficult with the advent of computers. It is still possible to tamper with or destroy evidence that exists in electronic form. However, in order to cover up the alteration or destruction of electronic evidence properly, the assistance of a computer professional is often required. A conspiracy with another individual, however, carries additional risks and is typically avoided.[35]

---

32 Tape media used to store backups are generally very inexpensive. The risk/cost of recreating information is high. As well, computer systems sometimes malfunction. All these factors combine to create a mind set which is very adverse to erasing data.

33 Solicitor-client (communications between clients and their legal advisors) and litigation privilege (communication between clients, legal advisors and third parties who are assisting the legal advisor for the purposes of providing advice in respect of anticipated or actual litigation) protect the contents of certain documents from being disclosed during discovery, from being seized by the government during investigation of a crime or other offence or produced at trial for the benefit of the opposite party. However, if it can be shown that copies of a privileged document are distributed outside the circle of solicitor and client, then the protection provided by these types of privilege can be lost.

34 See interview with J. Feldman in "Background Briefing: The E-Files" Radio National (21 June 1998), online: <http://www.abc.net/au/m/talks/bbing/stories/s11184.htm>.

35 As a consequence, individual action by even a moderately proficient computer user will almost always leave some sort of trace or sign. In some cases, it may be possible to locate other copies of the destroyed or altered evidence, or at least reconstruct portions.

1.3 E-MAIL AND DISCOVERY

E-mail messages have played a prominent role in several high profile cases.

During the US Congressional investigation of the Iran-Contra affair, investigators discovered many e-mail messages on backup computer tapes whose contents contradicted Oliver North's testimony. Apparently, he thought they were deleted and was unaware that copies existed on backup tapes.

Another high profile case was in respect to the Rodney King beating, where an e-mail message written by Los Angeles police officer Lawrence Powell on a miniature computer installed in his squad car was introduced at trial. The message contained a passage that read, "Oops. I haven't beat anyone so bad in a long time." The response from a second squad car not at the scene was "Oh not again. Why [did] you do that? Thought you agreed to chill out for a while."[36]

E-mail messages also helped play a crucial role in a dispute involving Atlantic Richfield Co.'s (Arco) sale of its solar energy subsidiary to Siemens Solar Industries (Siemens).[37] Following the sale, e- mails written by Arco employees were discovered stating that Arco would have had significant problems in successfully moving the technology from the laboratory to manufacturing and that "as it appears that [Arco's technology] is a pipe dream, let Siemens have the pipe". This helped show that at the time of the transaction, Arco knew its technology was not commercially viable and supported Siemen's allegations that Arco had misrepresented the ability of its subsidiary to develop the technology.

A trial in the fall of 1998 involving the United States Justice Department and 20 states against Microsoft was the first major trial to use e-mail as evidence. During the trial, the US government introduced e-mail that it claimed showed that Microsoft tried to push its rival, Netscape, into a deal to divide up the software browser market between the two. Microsoft also used e-mail messages as part of its defence—it subpoenaed e-mail records relating to an internal gripes list from rival Netscape to show that Netscape employees had criticized their management for making bad decisions in designing and shipping its browser.[38]

While e-mail evidence has been used in a number of such high profile cases, its predominant use has been in cases involving employment related disputes, includ-

---

36 See "In Messages, Officers Banter After Beating in Los Angeles" *The New York Times* (19 March 1991) A1.

37 See *Siemens Solar Industries v. Atlantic Richfield Co.*, Civ. No. 93-1126, 1994 WL 86368 (S.D.N.Y., 1994).

38 Netscape's internal e-mail list provides a good example of where unguarded comments and internal complaints, when viewed by outsiders, while not showing wrongdoing may nevertheless cause harm to a company's reputation.

ing wrongful dismissal, discrimination and sexual harassment.[39] An example of these is *Strauss v. Microsoft Corp.*,[40] which involved a motion by the defendant, Microsoft, for an order granting it partial summary judgment (to dismiss) in an employment discrimination action involving claims of gender discrimination. Strauss had been hired as an assistant to the technical editor of the Microsoft Systems Journal. As a result of Microsoft's failure to promote her to the technical editor position, when that position had become vacant, Strauss sued alleging gender discrimination.

One of four factors submitted as evidence of discrimination based on gender was inappropriate behaviour in the office by the publisher/editor, namely making comments and sending e-mail messages that were offensive to women. Examples of such inappropriate behaviour included:

- comments to the plaintiff that he was "president of the amateur gynecology club";
- sending an e-mail message to the entire Journal staff about "Mouse Balls", that contained sexual innuendo about male genitalia;
- sending an e-mail message directly to the plaintiff entitled "Alice in UNIX Land", that mixed computer language with sexual innuendo; and
- sending two other sexually explicit e-mail messages to one Journal employee who subsequently sent the material to the rest of the Journal staff.

Microsoft's motion to dismiss was denied. The court found that, when view in light of the plaintiff's other evidence of pretext, the publisher/editor's inappropriate behaviour in the office "could lead a reasonable jury to conclude that Microsoft's proffered reason is not the true reason for its failure to promote Strauss."

1.4 CONCLUSION

The discovery of electronic evidence has become the modern litigator's newest tool (or some would say, weapon). Lawyers and government investigators need to develop the knowledge and skill necessary to take advantage of the information residing in electronic form. From the perspective of lawyers, a good understanding of the technology and associated terminology is important so that the lawyer can:

- properly target the specific types and sources of electronic evidence that may exist, rather than having to use more general terminology which may more easily be answered without disclosing the sought-after evidence;

---

39 I.C. Ballon, "How Companies Can Reduce the Costs and Risks Associated with Electronic Discovery" *Computer Law* 15:7 (July 1998) 8. See cases previously cited in section 1.1.

40 814 F.Supp. 1186, 1993 U.S. Dist. LEXIS 1919, 65 Fair Empl.Prac.Cas. (BNA) 620, 64 Empl. Prac. Dec. P42,915 (S.D.N.Y., 1993).

- adequately understand the responses; and
- pose follow up questions more appropriately tied to previous responses.

This does not mean that lawyers and government investigators need to become computer specialists, but rather, that they need to understand enough about the technology to ask the right questions and enlist the assistance of forensic computer experts where necessary.[41] Lawyers who choose to ignore these new developments could expose themselves to malpractice claims.[42]

---

41 The assistance of a computer forensic expert possessing a current understanding of how specific software programs operate and manipulate data, can help a lawyer more accurately locate and utilize all relevant electronic data.

42 See Chester, "Must Litigators use Computers or Face Malpractice?" *Winning with Computers, Trial and Practice in the 21st Century* (Tredennick & Eidelman eds., *1991*).

2

Discovery of Electronic Evidence

This chapter presents a general overview of the steps involved in the discovery of electronic evidence. However, the specific steps and considerations may differ depending on whether the case involves a civil proceeding or a criminal prosecution.

2.1 TYPICAL STEPS IN THE DISCOVERY OF ELECTRONIC EVIDENCE

1. Determine if electronic data may play a role in the dispute.

    - Assess whether the opposing party may have evidence in electronic form that would be useful to the case or investigation.
    - Assess if your client has electronic data that may play a role. Also, advise your client to take immediate steps to preserve such data.[1]

2. Find out what hardware and software is utilized by the other party. An initial profile can be developed without revealing an express interest. For instance:

    - The other party's staff may have talked about their system at various conferences or written articles that contain a description.
    - A computer or industry publication may have run an article featuring the company and may have talked about its computer system.

---

1 Computer disks and tape media should be write-protected and appropriately labelled. A working copy of the files should be made and the originals stored in a secure location. A special "mirror" or "image" backup may need to be made of all computer hard disks which may contain, or may in the recent past have contained, relevant data.

- The vendor, who sold the other party its system or a component, may list that party in its press releases.

3.   Develop a strategic plan for the discovery of the electronic data.

- Determine who should be targeted early in the discovery process, in order to obtain the necessary additional information about the other party's system, to ensure all relevant electronic sources are covered.
- Determine what other persons or entities may have computer systems that contain relevant data (parent company, subsidiaries, home computers, laptops, third party service providers, consultants, time-sharing service bureau, etc.).
- Develop a plan to respond to requests for electronic data from the other party (if not already developed prior to the particular dispute).
- Consider whether an oral discovery should take place in a location where the other party will have access to its computer system and, therefore, be better able to provide responsive answers.
- Consider whether there is a reasonable risk that the opposing party will destroy evidence and, if so, make an appropriate motion for a preservation order.[2]

4.   Serve the other party with an initial notice letter as soon as possible.[3] Consider whether to send the letter prior to the commencement of formal litigation, or a full investigation, in order to put the other party on notice that relevant evidence may be destroyed if appropriate steps are not taken to preserve such evidence.

- Set out that you consider electronic data to be an invaluable source of evidence in the dispute or investigation. Specific examples should be given, including:[4]
  - data stored in a computer or other electronic device,
  - data stored on removable magnetic or optical media (*e.g.*, magnetic tape, floppy disks, and recordable optical disks),
  - e-mail,
  - data used for electronic data interchange,
  - audit trails,
  - digitalized pictures and video (*e.g.*, data stored in MPEG, JPEG, and GIF formats),
  - digitalized audio (*e.g.*, data stored in MP3, WAV, RealAudio and other formats), and
  - voicemail.

---

2 In a civil action, see Rule 45.01(1) of the *Rules of Civil Procedure* (Ontario) (the "Rules of Civil Procedure" or the "Rules").
3 For sample language, see <http://www.forensic.com/documents/warning.htm>.
4 See Overly, *supra*, at Chapter 1, note 8.

- Provide the other party with notice that they may destroy certain forms of electronic evidence through normal use of their computer system or other equipment unless they take immediate steps to preserve it.
- Request that the other party immediately create two complete and verified image copies of all potentially relevant electronic data (preferably on read-only media, such as CD-ROM).
- Advise the other party that off-the-shelf backup software and/or their current backup procedures may not be adequate to capture a copy of all relevant electronic data and that specialized software and expertise may be required.
- Set out as specifically as possible the types of information to be preserved and the possible locations where such evidence may exist.[5]

In some cases, it may be prudent to consider seeking a preservation order to protect against alteration or deletion of relevant electronic evidence.

5.   Implement the plan developed for the discovery of the electronic data.

- Use a series of written questions (interrogatories) to collect technical information regarding the other party's computer systems and procedures,[6] if permitted by the rules of law of the jurisdiction.
- Follow up with oral discovery (deposition) of the information systems department staff if permitted by the rules of law of the jurisdiction.
- Ensure that all requests for production clearly specify that electronic documents in addition to paper documents are being requested. It is advisable to include a very thorough and comprehensive definition of what is requested.
- Following receipt of electronic data, request any additional information required to properly analyze the data (for instance, identify the programs used to create or manipulate the data).
- Seek any electronic version of data referred to by a testifying expert.
- Consider whether it will be necessary to inspect or search the relevant computer system or whether it will be possible to rely on the electronic evidence that is disclosed by the other party.

---

5 People frequently forget about or are not aware of information contained in their computers. A general request for production, even one that specifically asks about documents stored in electronic form, may not elicit all the relevant material.

6 In the United States, this may be done through a demand for disclosure under Rule 26 of the *Federal Rules of Civil Procedure.* In some jurisdictions, an affirmative obligation on parties to identify relevant documents in the affidavit of documents must be provided to the opposing side. In Ontario, Rule 30.03(1) of the *Rules of Civil Procedure* requires a party to an action, within 10 days of the close of pleadings, to serve every other party with an affidavit of documents, disclosing to the full extent of the party's knowledge information and belief all documents relating to any matter in issue in the action that are or have been in the party's possession, control or power.

Early consideration of electronic discovery of data in the possession or under the control of an opponent can mean action can be taken to prevent relevant data from being destroyed. However, early consideration of electronic evidence in one's own party's possession is also important. If appropriate action is not taken, favourable evidence may be inadvertently destroyed. Early consideration of one's own data may also produce evidence that is relevant to that party's consideration of its own case. Additional lead time will also provide that party with time it may need to properly review any electronic evidence it may need to later disclose for portions that may contain privileged or confidential information.

In a case where each of the parties may have an interest in seeking discovery of electronic evidence from the other, they may have a mutual interest in reaching agreement on ground rules for the identification and disclosure of such evidence. Such an agreement, or stipulation, may confirm that:[7]

- each party will identify and otherwise treat electronic evidence in the same manner as any other type of evidence for the purpose of a party's disclosure;
- each party will immediately make and preserve complete and verified image backups of all electronic evidence that may be relevant;
- in respect of each record, the relevant party will fully identify the record, its location and the method of and schedule applicable to any backup of such record;
- each party will provide information about application programs used in recording, manipulating or storing any electronic records;
- each party will provide copies of all relevant electronic evidence in its native electronic form;
- each party will instruct its expert witnesses to retain complete copies of all versions of electronic data used or relied upon by such expert;
- each party will permit informal interviews of the other party's technical personnel;
- each party will permit the other party, including the other party's experts, to inspect its electronic records at its site, at such time that inspection will not unreasonably interfere with that party's business operations;
- any person given access to the other party's electronic evidence shall execute appropriate non-disclosure agreements; and
- neither party shall use an expert where there may be an existing conflict of interest.

---

7 Summarized from J.L. Kashi, "How to Conduct On-Premises Discovery of Computer Records", (ABA TechShow 99, Chicago, 18 March 1999).

2.2 SEARCH/SEIZURE OF COMPUTER SYSTEMS

(a) Important Considerations in the Conduct of the Search/Seizure

(i) *Searches*

A physical inspection of the other party's computer system may be permitted by various rules of civil procedure.[8] Of course, even though there is the possibility that a physical examination will turn up useful evidence, this must be balanced with the cost of such an examination.

Ideally, any search should be conducted by a neutral third party computer forensic expert. Such a party can typically conduct a more comprehensive examination. Also, where concerns regarding confidentiality are raised, such a party can be asked to execute appropriate non-disclosure agreements which can govern the type of information that may be disclosed to the discovering party. Use of a neutral expert may also reduce the likelihood of claims that the system or data of the party being examined were damaged as a result of the examination.

Alternatively, where the value of a case does not justify the additional expense of hiring a computer expert, and where the search is to be conducted by the discovering party's counsel, a stipulation should be obtained from the other party to prevent future objections. It may also be preferable to have the examination conducted by another lawyer, a law clerk, or other employee of the firm so that the lawyer does not risk becoming a witness in the case.

It should be noted that other computers present in the search location may also possibly contain relevant evidence. For instance, in *Alliance and Leicester Building Society v. Ghahremani*,[9] the defendant gave evidence that different versions of the same crucial document existed in different directories on the same computer. The defendant also gave evidence that it was the practice of the firm to make copies or backups of various documents by copying them from one computer to another, so that they would exist simultaneously on all the firm's computers. This was done in order to allow more than one secretary to work on the same documents at the same time.

---

8 For instance, see Cal. Civ. Proc. Code § 2031(a)(2). See Rule 35 of the *Federal Rules of Civil Procedure*. See also Rule 34(a) which provides, in part: "Any party may serve on any other party a request ... (2) to permit entry upon the designated land or other property in the possession or control of the party upon whom the request is served for the purpose of inspection and measuring, surveying, photographing, testing, or sampling the property or any designated object or operation thereon, within the scope of Rule 26(b)."

9 [1992] R.V.R. 198 (Eng. Ch. Div.).

Also, in the case of a search of a computer system that includes a network file server or which is operating a sophisticated operating system, the discovering party's computer expert will need to be given full "supervisory", "root" or "administrator" rights to the network file server. Without such rights, certain files and directories may not be visible.

(ii) *Seizures*

In some cases, a seizure of electronic evidence and/or the computer systems containing relevant evidence may be authorized by a warrant in a criminal investigation or an *Anton Piller*[10] order issued in a civil proceeding.[11] An example involving the latter was *Nintendo of America Inc. v. Coinex Video Games Inc.*,[12] where such an order was issued against numerous defendants. The requirements that had to be met were:[13]

1.   an extremely strong *prima facie* case;
2.   actual or potential damage to applicant must be very serious; and
3.   clear evidence that defendants have possession of incriminating documents or things and a real possibility exists that these may be destroyed before an application *inter partes* can be made.

The court also referred to a less onerous test adopted by the Court of Appeal in England in the subsequent decision of *Yousif v. Salama*,[14] where Lord Justice Brightman (at page 408) stated:

---

10   Refers to an *ex parte* order, issued if certain conditions are met, that permits the plaintiff to enter the defendant's premises to search, locate and remove relevant files. See *Anton Piller KG v. Manufacturing Process Ltd.*, [1976] 1 Ch. 55 (Eng. Ch. Div.).

11   For an example of a case where an *ex parte* seizure order was obtained to acquire electronic evidence in connection with a trade secret dispute, see *First Technology Safety Systems, Inc. v. Depinet*, 11 F.3d 641 (6th Cir. (Ohio), 1993). However, the order was subsequently reversed because the Sixth Circuit held that an applicant for *ex parte* relief must do more than assert that the adverse party would dispose of evidence if given notice. It was necessary to demonstrate that the adverse party has a history of disposing of evidence or violating court orders or that persons similar to the adverse party have such a history.

12   (1982), [1983] 2 F.C. 189 (Fed. C.A.).

13   *Supra*, at note 10. In that case, the plaintiff wished to restrain the defendant from infringing copyright, using the confidential information or making copies of their machines. However, the plaintiff was afraid that the defendant, if notified, would take steps to destroy the documents or would send them out of the jurisdiction so that there would be none in existence by the time the action reached the discovery stage. The plaintiff made an *ex parte* application for an order requiring the defendant to permit the plaintiff to enter the defendant's premises in order to inspect, remove or make copies of documents belonging to the plaintiff.

14   [1980] 3 All E.R. 405 (Eng. C.A.).

In my view the order sought in this case is justified if, but only if, there is prima facie evidence that essential documents are at risk. If essential documents are at risk, then it seems to me that this court ought to permit the plaintiff to take such steps as are necessary to preserve them.

So there are two questions to be asked. First, are the documents sought to be seized essential to the plaintiff's case? If so, are such documents at serious risk? Might they be dishonestly destroyed?

The following issues should be considered in respect of the conduct of a search and seizure:[15]

- If there is reason to believe that a computer may be found on the premises, the warrant or order should be drafted to allow seizure of the computer, computer media and any related equipment and evidence. This includes electronic or magnetic storage devices (such as, but not limited to, floppy disks, hard disks, removable storage media, CD-ROM and other magnetic or optical storage media, tape cartridges and magnetic tape reels, print buffer devices, PCMCIA cards), printers, as well as printouts.
- The fact that data stored on computer systems is capable of being destroyed quickly and easily suggest certain considerations in the execution of a search (such as, unannounced entry where there may be a motive to destroy the information and the need to quickly secure the premises).[16]
- The computer system should be disconnected from any network or remote access facility.
- Computer equipment should not be turned on. Simply turning on a computer-based system can cause an alteration of the electronic data contained within. At minimum, critical time stamps may be altered. A suspect may also have rigged the computer system to automatically delete incriminating data unless certain steps known only to that person are taken during the "boot up" process.[17]
- A suspect should not be permitted to power down his or her own system regardless of the arguments that are made. If a computer expert from the investigation team is not present then simply pull the plug.[18] If the suspect insists on assisting, ask them to write out the instructions they suggest be

---

15 Based, in part, on J. Berryhill, "Computer Forensics" *Police and Security News* (September 1997). See <http://www.computerforensics.com>.

16 J.A. Fontana, Chapter 23, "Computer-Related Searches" in *Law of Search and Seizure in Canada*, 4th Edition, (Toronto: Butterworths, 1997).

17 For instance, a computer may have been programmed to automatically delete critical data unless it is booted with a "safe" boot disk that contains startup instructions that override any destructive instructions stored on the computer's hard disk and executed by default.

18 It should be noted that certain operating systems may require a proper shut down. However, the risk posed by an improper shut down is lower than initiating a shut down procedure that may be booby-trapped.

followed and then pull the plug anyway. Their instructions may be helpful to later show that the suspect had attempted to destroy or tamper with evidence.

- Take pictures of and carefully label each cable and the specific "ports" on the computer where it was connected.
- Take other computer-related equipment that may contain electronic data that may be relevant to the case. This may include scanners, printers and digital cameras. Books and manuals may also be helpful to the investigating team's computer expert. Keep in mind those things that appear like audio, camcorder or video tapes may be used for storing computer data.
- Computer equipment and media should not be transported or stored anywhere that may expose them to temperature extremes.
- After the seizure, the investigating team's computer expert will lock the data or the media (either physically or electronically) to prevent alteration. Exact copies of the media (i.e., the computer's hard disk) will then be made with the analysis then usually performed on such copies (these are commonly called an image backup or a bit stream backup). This way, all interested parties can also obtain their own exact copies. Duplicate copies of the media should be made with care and using appropriate software to ensure the backup software itself does not alter the data (by creating log files or changing file attributes), and that the software captures all data including data that may have been deleted but not purged.
- A continuous chain of custody must be established and maintained. There is little point in finding useful evidence if it cannot subsequently be properly authenticated. This should include careful documentation of all steps involved in acquiring the electronic evidence.

A very different approach may be considered where a computer system is to be searched rather than seized, and where there is little likelihood that the operator will attempt to intentionally destroy data. In such cases, it may be preferable to instruct the party whose system is being searched to operate its own computer.

Also, in some situations, it will not be necessary or practical to conduct the search "on-site" or to remove the entire computer system. Factors which may dictate an off-site review include (i) the search may take substantial time and large numbers of personnel, so it may be more convenient to the targeted individual to have it done elsewhere; (ii) the number of experts and investigators available at any given time may be limited; or (iii) the number of on-site terminals and displays for conducting the search may be limited.[19] In such cases, it may be possible to download or copy the relevant evidence to media that can be removed and analyzed off-site. It is, therefore, important to take along equipment (such as parallel-port writeable storage devices) that can be used to store an image of any relevant electronic data.

Alternatively, in some circumstances, it may be possible to use backup equipment located at the search location to make any necessary copies, particularly if such

---

19   *Supra*, at note 16.

equipment is of a type that is compatible with the system used by the discovering/investigating party. Writeable CD-ROM drives are ideal for this purpose.

In either case, it will also be necessary to take along appropriate software that can make an exact image of a computer's hard disk. An example would be Power-Quest's *Drive Image Pro* (or in the case of file servers, *ServerMagic*). Once created, the first-generation backup copy should be write-protected and used to make second-generation copies that would be used for any analysis.

(b) Special Considerations in Criminal Investigations

A search for computer-related evidence may involve, and any search warrant should specify where applicable, items falling within one or more of the following categories:

- hardware (including computers);
- peripherals (such as printers, storage devices, communication devices, etc.);
- software;
- documentation in respect of the above; and
- electronically stored data.

In most cases, any computer-stored data that may be the object of the search will be stored on computer systems that are located at the physical premises intended to be searched. However, in some cases, the location being searched may contain a computer system that is only used to provide access to data that is stored on a different system located at a remote location.[20] While it is possible that the computer system located at the search location may contain local copies of the data, it would be advisable in such circumstances to obtain a search warrant that is broad enough to cover the remote computer system.

The most commonly occurring category of computer-related searches is the situation where law enforcement authorities seek to access and seize specific records, documentation or stored data from the memory of a suspect's computer, or a computer in the possession of a third party, as evidence of a crime. This is analogous to an entry pursuant to a search warrant to search filing cabinets for evidence, with the only difference being in the method of storage (*e.g.*, electronic rather than physical). A second category of computer-related searches concerns circumstances in which the computer itself is the instrument by which the crime has been committed. Examples include fraud, money laundering, distribution of pornography, and production of counterfeit cheques, identification and bills of exchange. Computers may also be utilized in the commission of a computer-related offence.[21]

---

20 Such access may take place through a private network or wide area network, through a dial-up facility using the public switched telephone network, or through the Internet.
21 *Supra*, at note 16.

In Canada, the *Criminal Code*[22] contains a number of provisions that expressly deal with searches of computer systems. Sections 487(2.1) and 487(2.2) provide:

> 487(2.1) A person authorized under this section to search a computer system in a building or place for data may
> (a)   use or cause to be used any computer system at the building or place to search any data contained in or available to the computer system;
> (b)   reproduce or cause to be reproduced any data in the form of a print-out or other intelligible output;
> (c)   seize the print-out or other output for examination or copying; and
> (d)   use or cause to be used any copying equipment at the place to make copies of the data.

> 487(2.2) Every person who is in possession or control of any building or place in respect of which a search is carried out under this section shall, on presentation of the warrant, permit the person carrying out the search
> (a)   to use or cause to be used any computer system at the building or place in order to search any data contained in or available to the computer system for data that the person is authorized by this section to search for;
> (b)   to obtain a hard copy of the data and to seize it; and
> (c)   to use or cause to be used any copying equipment at the place to make copies of the data.

Similar provisions may also be present in other quasi-criminal legislation. For instance, see section 16 of the *Competition Act*.[23]

A number of important considerations for computer-based searches executed pursuant to search warrants are discussed by James A. Fontana in *Law of Search and Seizure in Canada*:[24]

2.3 CONFIDENTIALITY CONCERNS

The party whose system is to be examined will likely be concerned about protection of its confidential information and may seek a protective order[25] to prevent discovery of its system.[26] In such case, the party requesting the examination can argue that:

---

22   R.S.C. 1985, c. C-46.
23   R.S.C. 1985, c. C-34.
24   *Supra*, at note 16.
25   For instance, see Cal. Civ. Proc. Code § 2031(e).
26   See Chapter 7.

- a physical inspection is required in order to preserve electronic evidence that would otherwise be destroyed through normal operation of the system;
- it would suffer extreme financial hardship and prejudice if denied access to the other party's computer system;[27] and/or
- it would be willing to enter into a non-disclosure agreement to protect the information from disclosure or other use, or that a neutral and independent expert could be appointed to perform the inspection and then only report on relevant information that is discovered.

2.4 PRESERVATION OF EVIDENCE

A party that is under a duty to preserve evidence or that has been served with an order to preserve evidence will have to immediately take certain steps to ensure that relevant evidence is not unintentionally deleted in the normal course of its operations. Such steps include:

- ensuring the computer system is not turned on;
- taking any actions that may be available to "write protect" the media. In the case of hard disk drives, this can usually be accomplished by disconnecting an appropriate wire on the signal cable that connects to the hard disk drive to the computer system;
- making arrangements to ensure that any backup of the media that is made does not alter the media[28] and that all data is backed up (*i.e.*, deleted data that may still be recoverable);
- until appropriate backups are created, (i) system maintenance activities such as de-fragmenting and compression should be discontinued;[29] and (ii) new software and data should not be installed or saved on a storage media that already contains data as this may result in overwriting data that may need to be preserved;
- ensuring that appropriate virus protection software and techniques are employed; and
- not reusing backup tapes or other media that may contain evidence that may need to be preserved.

---

27 Such an argument is most effective in cases that involve a large quantity of data and where such data is already available in electronic form in the opponent's computer system. See *State, By Humphrey v. Philip Morris, Inc.*, 1998 WL 257214 (Minn.Dist.Ct., 1998).

28 By default, many backup programs alter file attribute information.

29 On some systems, these activities are performed automatically at scheduled periods and must be manually turned off.

2.5 USE OF A FORENSIC EXPERT

This section and the one that follows discuss the use of a computer forensic expert. In some cases, it may be advantageous to utilize two different individuals for this purpose. One expert (the "litigation assistant") could be used to advise the party, while the second expert (the "expert witness") could be used to carry out any investigatory work that may be required. This second expert would then be free to testify at trial while the work of the expert retained to provide litigation assistance could continue to be protected under rules relating to privilege.

(a) Pre-Litigation/Investigation Risk Reduction

Information in a client's computer system that is no longer useful to the client may become a liability. Prior to the commencement of any litigation involving electronic data, a lawyer working with a professional consultant knowledgeable about electronic evidence can assist his or her client in the design and implementation of an electronic data management and retention program.[30] The consultant should ideally be retained by the lawyer in order to ensure maximum protection of the consultant's work under rules of privilege.

Pre-litigation defensive services may include:[31]

- compiling an inventory of the organization's electronic data (what is there and where it is);
- compiling a list of relevant privacy and confidentiality policies affecting such electronic data for review by legal counsel;
- development of "style guides" for business communications;
- development of guidelines for the retention and destruction of electronic data (in consultation with the organization's legal counsel);
- staff training regarding electronic data risk;
- assistance with the design and conduct with periodic audits; and/or
- implementation assistance in respect of the above.

The consultant can also assist with the development of cost-effective methodologies or systems for responding to potential discovery requests for electronic data. Clients without a pre-existing and cost-effective system for responding to discovery requests can incur significant costs if called upon to produce or preserve electronic data.

---

30 *The Manual for Complex Litigation*, 2nd ed. (Toronto: CCH, 1985) in 21.461 at 75 states that an attorney "may require assistance . . . in formulating precise questions and the answering party may need time and special guidance to respond".

31 For instance, see the list of electronic risk control services provided by Computer Forensics Inc. at <http://www.forensics.com/services/risk.htm>. See Chapter 6 for a more detailed review of defensive strategies.

(b) After Commencement of Litigation/Investigation

After commencement of litigation, a lawyer or government investigator may also need to retain an expert in the field of electronic evidence to provide assistance in collecting, preserving, analyzing and presenting computer-related or other electronic evidence. More particularly, such an expert can help in:

- determining whether or not electronic data may play a role in the litigation;
- identifying the potential sources of electronic data in the client's and the opposing party's computer systems;
- preparing a strategy to get the other party's electronic information (including identifying custodians of electronic data);
- providing assistance in drafting affidavits and search warrants;
- providing assistance in seizing computer systems;
- advising on the preservation of electronic evidence;
- assisting in drafting a letter to the opposing party prior to the commencement of an action, or as soon as possible thereafter, to provide the opposing party with notice of possible sources of relevant electronic data, the fact that such information may be destroyed unless immediate steps are taken to preserve it and that such destruction may result in sanctions being imposed by the court;[32]
- developing a strategic plan for the acquisition of the electronic data on the opposing party's computer system;
- drafting a request for production of electronically stored records;
- assisting in the development of interrogatories (if available in the jurisdiction), questions for witnesses and other production requests;
- assisting in the examination for discovery (deposition, in the United States) of MIS/IT staff;
- anticipating and responding to objections made by the other party;[33]
- responding to requests from the opposing party for electronic data (this may include:
    - suggestions on cost-effective means for responding to discovery requests with minimal disruption to business operations; and
    - formulating objections);
- retrieving and/or recovering hidden electronic data from either party's computer system;[34]

---

32 A duty to preserve evidence may not arise unless the party possessing the evidence has notice of its relevance. Such a letter will put the opposing party on notice that certain forms of evidence may be relevant and that its failure to change its normal business operations and practices may lead to the destruction of such evidence.

33 For example, the other party may argue that the discovery request is too burdensome. In such instances, a forensic expert can help review whether the other party's claimed costs are inflated.

34 A third party expert can serve a useful role in searching the opposing party's computer system for relevant data if there are reasonable suspicions that a party may be withholding relevant information. If required by the other party, this expert can be placed under a duty not to disclose confidential or proprietary information not relevant to the case or

- providing special software to preserve electronic evidence;[35]
- providing special tools and utilizing special techniques, if necessary, to review[36] or extract[37] the relevant information from electronic data provided by the other party;
- reconstructing usage of or access to a particular system based on forensic analysis of system log files and other electronic data;
- helping to ensure that relevant evidence is adequately protected and a proper chain of custody established;
- determining the accuracy and authenticity of electronic evidence;
- conducting investigations of factors that may raise questions about the reliability of electronic evidence, including reviewing the integrity of the file allocation table and data storage areas where electronic data is stored;
- providing testimony as an expert witness at trial to establish the necessary foundation for the introduction of electronic evidence; and/or
- educating the court regarding technology.

The use of a forensic expert may also be useful, or even required, for the purposes of searches/seizures conducted pursuant to search warrants.[38] According to Fontana:[39]

> Implicit in the search of computers will be the necessity of using experts to access and identify the material described in the warrant, a fact which should be recited in the search warrant information. The use of experts will serve a number of purposes:
> (1) quick access to the material before it can be destroyed;
> (2) proper identification of the targeted material;

---

information that is protected by privilege.

35 Commercial off-the-shelf backup programs do not normally capture copies of files that have been deleted but may still be recoverable. Many other types of potentially useful electronic evidence discussed in this publication may also not be captured.

36 Electronic data can be reviewed using full-text search software, by arranging the files chronologically according to the date they were created or last modified or through the preparation of vocabulary lists of all the words used that can then be reviewed for the names of certain parties or other keywords relevant to the case. Where electronic files are stored on a multi-user computer system or local area network, they can also be reviewed by grouping them according to the name of the computer user who last modified the file (the "owner"). Other services may also be available to assist in extracting relevant information from large data sets.

37 Electronic data might not be viewable without access to the software used in its creation or other special tools that can import and display documents stored in proprietary formats. Assistance may also be required to break passwords in order to access or decrypt certain types of data.

38 A police officer may have the assistance of persons, who are neither named in the warrant nor peace officers, provided that the police officer remains in control of and accountable for the search. *R. v. B. (J.E.)* (1989), 52 C.C.C. (3d) 224 (N.S. C.A.)

39 *Supra*, at note 16.

(3) avoidance of the removal of innocent material;
(4) compliance with any limits or conditions set out in the warrant;
(5) avoidance of unnecessary damage;
(6) dealing with material that has been encrypted or "concealed" within the system.

It is suggested that a pre-execution briefing by the investigators may assist all the participants, including the officers, experts and other search personnel, in gaining a better understanding of the items described in the warrant.

A forensic expert may employ a third party data recovery service to assist with the search and recovery of electronic evidence. However, this will typically not be necessary unless there is a serious problem with the storage device. Many minor problems can be corrected using commercially available software such as Encore Software's *Hard Drive Mechanic*[40] or PowerQuest's *Lost and Found.*[41]

2.6 SELECTING A COMPUTER FORENSIC EXPERT

The following should be considered when selecting a computer forensic expert:

- Look for someone knowledgeable in the legal nuances involved in dealing with electronic data as evidence. The task requires more than expertise in retrieving electronic data. An adverse party may claim the evidence has been tampered with. Proper procedures and protocols must be followed to ensure the evidence will be admissible.[42]
- The individual could be called to testify in court to explain what he or she did to retrieve and analyze the data. That individual's own level of experience and training (and not just that of his or her employer) may become relevant. Prior experience in testifying in court may be helpful.

---

40 This program repairs and restores hard disk drives after a software related crash. See <http://www.encoresoftware.com>.

41 This program automatically recovers and restores data after an accidental or intentional data loss, or from corrupt media caused by a disk crash or logical system failure. According to the vendor, the software will even recover data if the partition has been reformatted or if the file allocation tables have been destroyed. See <http://www.pow-erquest.com>.

42 For instance, Ontrack Computer Evidence Services utilizes its *Ontrack Forensic Protocol*™, a set of procedures that addresses security, authenticity and the chain of custody of the preserved evidence. The use of the protocol is designed to preserve the recovered evidence in its original form, avoid authenticity objections and streamline the process of admitting recovered evidence into evidence. Other professional computer forensics service providers have developed similar procedures.

- Check references. Also, as this field matures, industry certification may become more important.
- Look for data recovery capabilities that can handle the specific systems and media that are relevant to the case. In some cases, this will require access to computer hardware and application software that is no longer commercially available.[43]
- Specialized tools developed for analyzing data from specific application programs can make a big difference when access is required to data stored in proprietary formats or when search capabilities are required. This is particularly relevant to e-mail or any other data that may be stored in a proprietary format.

2.7 COST OF COMPUTER DATA RECOVERY SERVICES

The total cost of utilizing the services of a computer data recovery service may depend on a number of variables:[44]

- *Project Lead Times.* Short project lead times typically result in higher costs.
- *Resource Requirements.* This factor is related to project lead time. Heavy resource requirements, particularly if placed upon a smaller computer forensic service with limited resources, may result in higher costs. Even in the case of larger computer forensic services, the use of a greater number of people, necessitated by short lead times, usually means additional time required to coordinate activities.
- *Type of Storage Media.* Data recovery from hard drives with industry standard interfaces is usually straightforward and relatively inexpensive. Data recovery from devices with non-standard interfaces and from removable storage media (such as tapes, cartridges and removable hard drives) where access to the applicable drive is not available is more expensive.
- *Volume of Data.* More data usually means higher total costs, although per unit cost should drop with larger jobs.
- *Operating Systems.* Data recovery from certain operating systems such as Microsoft *Windows* and *DOS* may be less expensive than other operating systems such as UNIX or *Windows NT*.
- *Data Format.* Recovery of data stored in a proprietary format or encrypted format requires an additional step and may require use of custom software.

---

43 The same company may provide expertise in both computer forensic services and data recovery. Alternatively, a computer forensic consultant may subcontract any data recovery tasks to a third party data recovery service.

44 See also, Ontrack Computer Evidence Service, "Electronic Evidence: Cost Management and Reduction" online: <http://www.ontrack.com/os/ce_4.asp>.

Costs may be significantly higher if the data recovery service does not have access to such customized software developed for a prior job or if its staff are not familiar with the particular data format.

- *Condition of Media.* Damaged media will require additional steps (and associated costs) before recovery of the desired evidence can be commenced.

3

Sources of Electronic Evidence / Where to Look

In order to conduct a comprehensive search for electronic evidence, lawyers and investigators need to learn where to search and what to look for. They need to determine what computer systems and what software applications on these systems may contain electronic data. They will also need to verify the integrity of any electronic data that are found.

While the questions that follow are geared for use in respect of commonly used computer and other equipment typically used in a business environment, a similar line of questioning should be pursued for any specialized equipment used in the particular business or industry. For instance, in a medical malpractice case where magnetic resonance imaging (MRI) photographs are produced, it may be useful to ascertain whether other images were taken but not printed. These may be retained in the MRI unit or in the hospital's picture archive system.

3.1 PEOPLE AND WORKFLOW

- Identify key individuals and the workflow between them:
  - ascertain how each individual uses his or her computer;[1]
  - include secretaries and assistants;
  - keep in mind that documents drafted by a key party or witness may be stored on an assistant's computer; and

---

1 Data that has been selectively saved to diskette or other removable media should not be overlooked. Users often store backup copies of files onto floppy diskettes. These may not be produced or disclosed (*i.e.*, listed in the affidavit of documents) because they were considered to be "personal" backups. It may, therefore, be important to ask the "right" questions.

- find out if the key party or witness normally dictates his or her memos and letters to a voice recorder or directly to a PC equipment with voice dictation software.
- Request a list of all files or records created or modified by the relevant individuals during the relevant time period.
- Ascertain the identity of people who had access to relevant documents. Include any third parties that may have been provided with copies.
- Determine how and where records are maintained, distributed and destroyed:
  - where and with whom copies or versions of documents reside;
  - the computer resources to which these individuals had access; and
  - the type of connectivity that exists between these computer resources and others in the organizations (*i.e.*, e-mail, local area network, etc.).

3.2 COMPUTER HARDWARE AND OTHER EQUIPMENT

Multiple copies of electronic evidence are easy to create and distribute. In many cases, multiple copies exist in a number of locations so that other copies may still be found even if the responding party believes that all copies have been previously erased.

In developing a strategy for the discovery of electronic data, litigators or investigators and their forensic expert need to consider all the possible locations that may contain a copy of the relevant information. These locations may include:

- office PCs;
- diskettes;
- network file server or mainframe computer systems;
- home PCs;
- pocket organizers including *Windows CE* computers and palm pilot devices;
- handheld digital dictation recorders;
- home caller display devices;[2]
- shared departmental laptop computers;
- computer resources under the control of an outside entity:
  - software or data held in escrow by a third party
  - software or data held by other third parties, such as contractors or consultants
  - software or data licensed to third parties
  - transmission logs maintained by third parties (*i.e.*, pager companies, phone companies providing wired or wireless service);

---

2 Many of these will store the last 10, 50 or even 100 phone numbers to have placed calls to that location.

- e-mail or communication[3] gateways;
- pagers and wireless phones;[4]
- fax machines[5] or network fax servers; or
- backup copies of the above sources.

For each of these computer systems, it would be useful to identify the make and model of the computer, the operating system being utilized, application programs installed, names of operators or administrators, applicable backup procedures, password protection and other security mechanisms, and maintenance history.

In addition, computer systems or their components are sometimes moved around within organizations or replaced due to failures.[6] Confirm that the possible relevant systems being targeted for a search are the actual equipment that was utilized during any relevant time period. Many organizations label each PC with an asset number so that it may be tracked on fixed asset reports.

Personal computers store information in a number of locations, including:

- random access memory ("RAM") that is erased each time the computer is turned off or restarted (but may contain useful information if a computer system is seized during a raid);
- hard disks (one or more);
- removable storage media (such as floppy disks, CD-ROMs, cartridges and tapes); and
- CMOS memory (stores configuration information, that may include a password required to access the system).

---

3 An Internet proxy server may contain useful logs or on-line activity and may also have cached copies of recently accessed information.

4 Check the pager's memory and speed dial numbers programmed into the wireless phone. Some wireless phones keep track of recently called numbers or phone numbers that recently called that phone. Some PCS or cellular service operators provide voicemail and fax reception services.

5 Almost all fax machines capture and store electronic logs of reception and transmission activities. In most cases, such logs may automatically print (and be purged) once a certain number of transactions have accumulated. Also, many fax machines use rolls of film that are consumed in the printing process. In such cases, these rolls may contain a copy of everything that has been printed on that machine, including received faxes, activity logs and cover pages corresponding to transmitted faxes. Many fax machines also contain memory to store outgoing faxes (and should therefore be immediately examined during any search of the premises).

6 In some cases it may even be possible to recover data from damaged storage devices such as hard disks. A number of data recovery services can provide the services of specially trained engineers, equipment and a "clean room" where a damaged hard disk can be taken apart, repaired and reassembled, or where the information contained may be otherwise extracted even in situations where the unit cannot be repaired.

Individual computers may also be connected together to form a network. Two types of networks can be constructed. The first is called a "peer-to-peer" network. Such networks do not include a central file server. Files can be stored on the hard disks of any computer attached to this type of network. Consequently, discovery may require an examination of the hard disk of every connected computer, or at least the ones that could be accessed (including access through the network) by the relevant employees.

The second type of network is called a "client-server" network and includes one or more central file servers. Users can store files either on the central file server or the hard disk in their local computer. Discovery of a client-server network (that is the most prevalent type in use) will require examination of the hard disks of local computers used by the relevant employees, as well as those of any file servers that could be accessed by such employees. In the case of an organization with offices in multiple locations, this may need to include file servers located in other offices if accessible to the relevant employees through a wide area network. It may be as easy for a particular employee to utilize a system thousands of miles away, or to distribute a message to such system, as it is to access a local file server.

In considering the possible locations where electronic evidence might be found, it is important to think globally rather than restricting thinking to the locations of the key individuals of the opposing party. Many large organizations have wide area networks that are augmented with gateways to the Internet and links to public e-mail or Electronic Data Interchange[7] (EDI) service providers.

In conjunction with a review of computer hardware that may potentially contain relevant evidence, it will be necessary to ascertain the applicable desktop and network/server operating systems used on such computer systems.

Although the foregoing focuses on computer-based sources of electronic information, non-computer sources should also be considered. For instance, in a case involving an automobile accident, useful information may have been captured in "black boxes" which track the speed of the vehicle, steering wheel position, whether the seatbelt was worn, whether the brakes were applied, etc.

3.3 APPLICATION SOFTWARE

Businesses may use a number of different software programs to store information. Each of these programs can be a potential source of evidence. These programs and the type of information they track include:

---

7   EDI is a series of standards which provide computer-to-computer exchange of business documents between different companies' computer systems over communication lines.

- word processing[8] or spreadsheet programs;[9]
- document management systems and features for tracking drafts;[10]
- e-mail;[11]
- groupware applications (*e.g.*, *Lotus Notes*);
- Web browser software (*e.g.*, Netscape *Navigator* and Microsoft *Explorer*);
- personnel records—both formal ones maintained by the organization and informal ones maintained by particular managers;[12]
- databases;[13]
- calendars;[14]
- to-do lists or bring-forward systems;
- electronic phone message slips;
- graphics and other multimedia presentation software;[15]

---

8 Prior drafts can be used to show elements of a negotiation or provisions agreed to during negotiations but missing from the executed version of an agreement.

9 An examination of the formulas and the optimization of cells can show implicit assumptions that were used to reach a certain result or conclusion, provide a better understanding of the relationship between the various data elements and permit the testing of different alternative scenarios.

10 A document management system may incorporate a feature that keeps track of when and by whom certain documents were modified or viewed.

11 E-mail messages are especially dangerous because, unlike other more formal written communication forms, people just sit down, write and send what they are thinking. E-mail conversations between peers can be especially candid about an organization's problems. People in the trenches sometimes say inappropriate things. E-mail is also often used for gossip that can be especially embarrassing in the event of an unfair dismissal action. Another factor that makes e-mail dangerous is the fact that most people believe that e-mail messages are not stored, or if they are then they are deleted periodically, when in fact most e-mail messages are stored for significant periods of time.

12 For instance, there are now several PC programs that can be used to manage people (*e.g.*, *ManagePro* from Advantos Performance Systems, Inc.) or assist in the drafting of performance reviews.

13 In a product liability case, customer complaint or technical support databases can be very useful to show when a company first acquired knowledge of a problem or defect. Service or parts inventory records can be used to identify how frequently a problem was occurring or a part was failing. After identifying relevant databases, the record format used in each should be requested so that a production request can be constructed that lists the relevant fields. A list of standard reports, that can be produced from each of these databases, should also be ascertained. It may also be possible to utilize third-party report generation programs to produce customized reports.

14 Note that some calendar programs will automatically move information that is older than a certain age from a main calendar file to an archive file and/or may give the user an option to delete the older information.

15 Presentation materials may have been used in a sales presentation and can show representations, outside of the written agreement, that were made by a party.

- financial and accounting systems;[16]
- financial analyses and projections;
- order and production information;
- EDI communications with suppliers and customers;
- computer-aided design and computer-aided manufacturing (CAD/CAM) systems, engineering drawings and data;[17]
- shipping receipts and transportation logs;[18]
- telephone records;[19]
- pager messages;[20]
- point-of-sale (POS) systems;
- scheduling and materials ordering systems;
- project management software;[21]
- *DOS* shell programs;[22]
- voice dictation programs;[23] or
- industry-specific vertical applications.

It is important to think broadly when considering the types of applications that may contain relevant evidence. For instance, if a computer belonging to a paedophile is being examined, evidence of child pornography would obviously be important to

---

16 An opponent's accounts receivable file will list past clients of the company and, in a contractual dispute, could be used to support a claim that the company did not have sufficient experience or competence to make certain contractual promises regarding performance or to undertake certain types of work. In a product liability situation, an examination of refunds to dissatisfied customers could be used to show that the other party had notice of a problem.

17 Designs stored in CAD/CAM manufacturing programs can show how a product was designed, its tolerances, other designs considered but not selected, and a chronology of the design process.

18 Shipping receipts can be very useful in toxic tort litigation. Also, some major transportation firms utilize systems that can track a particular truck's movements in real time. In many cases, this information might be archived and retained in electronic form.

19 Most business telephone systems track details about telephone calls including the identity of the caller, who was called and the duration. It may also track whether the call was an analog or digital call (*i.e.*, a modem call).

20 PC-based software to send messages to pagers has been available for some time. Such software typically creates a log file that stores the date and time of a page, who was paged and the full-text of the message sent.

21 Project management software can be especially useful in showing preventative or safety tasks that were subsequently removed to save time or money. Some programs in this category such as *Microsoft Project* allow users to save "baseline" project information for comparison to the then current version.

22 Many recent *Windows* users still like to "drop to *DOS*" to perform certain functions. A number of programs known as "*DOS* shells" are available to facilitate this task. Many track a certain number of historic *DOS* commands. For instance, one program, *Praxim*, allows scrolling through the last 30 command line commands that were issued. These could be used to show evidence of file deletion or copying.

23 Such programs may create audio files that contain a recording of recent dictation. They may also contain a list of custom words added to the system by the user.

the case. But so would evidence of communications with children, logs of access to children chat lines, alias names used to impersonate children, etc. Even computer games may be relevant if they were used to lure children. In some cases, computer games may even contain a list of names of players and their scores.[24]

3.4 OTHER QUESTIONS TO ASK

- What formal backup procedures were in place?
- What technical security mechanisms were in place to protect the integrity of information stored on the system?[25]
- What document retention programs were in place and were they actually adhered to prior to the commencement of the dispute?
- Was the data stored on the relevant computer systems managed by a document management system?[26]
- What information was preserved and how?
- What information was not preserved and why?
- What types of access records, log files and audit trails were created?[27] Did the employer utilize any special tools or software to monitor computer usage by employees?
- It is also important to collect information regarding the reliability of systems. Questions should, therefore, be asked regarding instances of computer viruses and incidents involving lost data or unauthorized access.

3.5 BACKUP POLICIES AND PROCEDURES

- What formal policies and procedures did the other party have related to backups?
- How often were routine backups made?
- What backup copies were made that relate to the time period in question?
    - Is the data still available from these backups?
    - Even if the data is no longer available, is the physical media that was used still available?
- Were other copies made as part of an *ad hoc*, informal or "personal" backup (on tapes or floppy disk) or printed out on paper?
- Are there other copies stored off-site or not in the company's possession?

---

24 From a "war story" told by Jon Berryhill of Berryhill Computer Forensics.

25 Companies may need to develop and implement specific procedures and access control mechanisms to prove that electronic data was not changed from the time of its creation.

26 A document management system could potentially contain audit or log files that could show a record of documents that were created, deleted, altered or viewed during the relevant time period.

27 For instance, a log of the subject line of a deleted and purged e-mail message could potentially be far more incriminating than the actual message may have been.

- What hardware equipment and software programs were used to make the backups?
- What types of logs and audit trails were created?
  - Are these logs still available?
  - Were copies of these logs stored on other backups (this would be useful to verify that no tampering had taken place).

3.6 ELECTRONIC MEDIA PRODUCTION

If the opposing party produces copies of electronic data, it is useful to ascertain:

- whether other copies, versions or drafts are also in existence;
- who had access to the data and who had an opportunity to modify the data;
- what security and access control mechanisms were in place to protect the data;
- positional information regarding the location of the files;[28] and
- any information about the file tracked by the operating system.[29]

It will be important to preserve the chain of custody of the evidence to ensure that a complete and reliable copy was made and that no data was added, deleted or changed from the time the copy was made to the time it is offered into evidence at trial.

---

28 Confirm that the file name was not modified and ascertain the disk and sub-directory where the file was located. Each of these can convey important information about the file.

29 For instance, *Windows* tracks the date and time each file was created, modified and last accessed. In the case of *Windows 95* and later versions, such information can be displayed by viewing the file's "properties".

4

Finding Hidden Sources of Electronic Evidence

4.1 FILES AND DIRECTORIES MARKED AS "HIDDEN"

An examination of a computer disk for files should include a search for any files marked as hidden. This attribute is commonly used to hide certain system files from normal view.[1] Files marked as hidden will not appear in normal directory listings. An entire sub-directory can also be marked as hidden and can be made to disappear from normal view.[2]

Hidden files and directories, however, will appear if special software is used to examine the file directory and are normally backed up to tape as part of a normal system backup. In *Windows 98*, hidden files and directories can be viewed by changing the default settings on the *Windows Explorer*.[3]

Also, sometimes during an abnormal shutdown of a computer system (particularly, a *DOS/Windows*-based system), the File Allocation Table (FAT) on the hard disk may not be properly updated, resulting in certain files, segments of files or even directory references become "lost". Certain utility programs (such as SCANDISK in the case of *Windows*) will search for and identify such data segments on the hard disk that are no longer properly referenced from the FAT. The user is then given

---

1 Examples of files that are marked as hidden by default include (i) *MS-DOS* boot files that are executed when a computer is first turned on, and (ii) the "swap" file used by *Windows*.

2 In *Windows 98*, a file or sub-directory (also known as a folder) can be hidden by setting the "hidden" attribute for that file or folder in *My Computer* or *Windows Explorer*. The "hidden" attribute can also be accessed by right-clicking on the specific file or folder and then clicking on *Properties*.

3 On the "View" menu, click on "Folder Options". Click on the "View" tab, and then click on "Show all files". The default attribute is not to show hidden or system files.

the option to either "delete" such data or save the data to the root directory (*i.e.*, "C:\") with a file name such as FILE0000.CHK.

4.2 "DELETED" INFORMATION IN COMPUTER STORAGE DEVICES

(a) The Recycle Bin

Many micro computer-based operating systems, such as Microsoft's *Windows*, utilize a "recycle bin", "trash can" or similar facility that is used to hold "deleted" files in a temporary holding area where they can be easily restored if necessary. The amount of disk space allocated for this function is typically limited and the oldest files are removed as newer "deleted" files are added. The recycle bin may be configured to automatically purge files after a set period of time or after a certain percentage of the hard disk is full. A user may also manually empty the recycle bin on an *ad hoc* basis or may selectively remove files from it. The recycle bin may also be disabled, and in such case, files are removed immediately.

Certain utility software may also install a second-level recycle bin that is also used to temporarily hold copies of deleted files. These types of programs may create a new folder on the computer's hard drive, and anytime a file is deleted, whether at the command line, in a 16-bit application, or by emptying the recycle bin, such software may store the files for a specified period before releasing them. While in this state, deleted files can usually be safely and completely restored.

(b) Deleted But Not Overwritten

Files that are deleted from systems that do not use a recycle bin or similar facility (as well as files that have been deleted from the recycle bin) may still be recoverable because of the nature of the computer disk storage mechanism. To understand how this is possible, it is useful to review how files are stored on a computer system.

The storage space available on a computer hard disk or floppy disk is divided into storage blocks or units called sectors.[4] Sets of sectors—usually between 2 and 8—are grouped into a "cluster".[5] Space is then allocated to files in units of clusters. A very small file may fit into a single cluster but typically multiple clusters are required to hold the contents of a single file. A directory, called the File Allocation

---

4   For example, the size of each disk block is selected when the hard disk is originally initialized and before any data is stored. The sector size for an *MS-DOS* formatted disk is 512 bytes.

5   For example, each cluster of an *MS-DOS* formatted disk will be between 1,024 and 4,096 bytes in size.

Table (FAT), is used to hold the names assigned to each file and keep track of the storage clusters in use by each file.

When a file on a computer hard disk or floppy diskette is deleted, the file is not actually erased. Instead, the information stored in the FAT is updated to indicate that the blocks that were in use by the deleted file are now available for re-use to store data belonging to new files.[6]

The reason that the file is not actually erased during the deletion operation is that data on a magnetic storage media can only be erased by recording new data on top of older data and doing so would impact the response time and performance of the computer system. A file is, therefore, not actually erased when deleted, but rather its entry in the FAT is marked as deleted, and the disk clusters formerly used to store its contents are marked as available for re-use.

In many instances, therefore, it is possible to use an "UNDELETE" command or a special utility program[7] to recover all or part of a previously deleted file if some or all of the clusters formerly used by that file have not been overwritten by new information. As previously mentioned, in some cases the computer may be running software that automatically moves all deleted files into a special storage location where they can be more easily and predictably recovered in event of accidental deletion.[8] The storage space occupied by these files is then released on a first-in first-out basis when new files need to be stored. Many network and desktop operating systems routinely provide this type of recovery facility.[9]

Even when every single cluster has been re-used, it is sometimes possible to recover remnants of older files. This is because the data stored in the last cluster used by a file will rarely exactly fill the entire cluster.[10] If the data written to the last cluster by a newer file is shorter than the data previously written to that cluster by the deleted file then a remnant of the deleted file may still exist.[11]

---

6 In *MS-DOS*, the first character in the file's directory entry is replaced with the hexbyte "E5", that identifies it as an erased file.

7 For example, Symantec Corp.'s *Norton Utilities* or *PC Tools* programs for PCs or *MacTools* for Macintosh or SofTouch System's *GammaTech Utilities* for OS/2.

8 For example, *MS-DOS*'s UNDELETE in "Delete Sentry" mode or the recycle bin feature in *Windows 95* and *Windows 98*.

9 For instance, the SALVAGE function in Novell *Netware*. In *Windows 95* and *Windows 98*, files that are deleted by moving their icons to the trash can, may be retained and recoverable until the trash can is emptied.

10 A file will not fill the last cluster unless its size is an exact multiple of the cluster size. For example, a file stored on a disk partitioned into a cluster of 1,024 bytes will not completely fill the last cluster unless the file size is 1,024 bytes or a multiple of 1,024 bytes (*i.e.*, 2,048, 4,096).

11 For example, assuming a cluster size of 2,048 bytes, a file containing 2,049 bytes would completely fill up one cluster and only one byte of the second storage cluster. Therefore, 2,047 bytes of the second cluster would not be overwritten and may still contain recoverable data from a previously deleted file.

It is more probable that the last cluster used by a new file was not also the last cluster used by a deleted file and, therefore, was entirely filled with data from the deleted file.[12] If on average, the new file fills half of the cluster with new data then the remaining half will still contain data from the older file. The size of the information that can be recovered can be, on average, between 512 bytes and 2,048 bytes.[13] If word processing formatting codes are taken into account then this amount of data could amount to between one-quarter and one full page of information.

The primary concern should probably be deleted files that are still recoverable. Information recovered from the trail ends of re-used storage blocks is usually small in size and difficult to put into any context as to its origin. In addition, the increasing use of real-time compression by newer versions of computer operating systems,[14] a feature in some network operating systems to erase deleted information,[15] and the ability of newer network operating systems[16] to sub-allocate disk blocks on file servers, will mean a decreased ability to recover useful information.

The same recovery potential may be possible with respect to a floppy diskette or computer hard disk that has been reformatted. In many cases, a utility program supplied with the operating system or sold by third parties may be available to recover the files that existed prior to the reformatting operation (assuming that the clusters that were used by those files had not been since re-used).[17] Even in situations where such an "unformat" operation is not possible, it may still be possible to search for information using a special utility program called a disk editor.

In some cases, even if a file and its data are completely erased, it may be possible to recover older versions of the file name. Prior to *Windows 95*, renaming a file would automatically overwrite the old name in the directory. Starting with *Windows 95*, renaming a file causes a new directory entry to be made and the old name is treated as an erased file with only its first character overwritten. The old name

---

12 If the last cluster used by a new file were also the last cluster used by a deleted file, then data from the deleted file would only be recoverable if their length were longer than the data stored in that cluster by the newer file.

13 Assuming cluster sizes of 1,024 to 4,096 bytes.

14 Available as part of the disk operating system in *MS-DOS* 6.0, *Windows 95* and higher versions and optional third party programs such as *Stacker*.

15 Novell *Netware* for instance would overwrite the information contained in a cluster used by a file that was actually erased. This would happen when the space used by that file was purged. Purging would occur either immediately (if so configured), when initiated by the file server administrator issuing a "PURGE" command, or when the space utilized by a deleted file is needed to store new information.

16 Such as Novell *Netware* 4.0 and above.

17 Early versions of *MS-DOS* did not support unformatting and disks formatted on a computer using such a version of the operating system cannot usually be recovered. Newer versions of *MS-DOS* added support for unformatting so that users who issued the FORMAT command by accident (and without using the /U parameter) can recover their data.

remains in the FAT directory (and can be recovered) until overwritten when the directory entry is required for a new file.[18]

Another potential source of data may be disk storage media that have malfunctioned. A diskette that generates a read error on a less tolerant disk drive may still be readable, or partially readable, on another disk drive. A hard disk that appears to be broken might still be fully readable if the malfunction is due to the "controller" circuitry and that part is subsequently replaced. Even where the problem with a hard disk is due to a more serious "head crash", the information may still be readable by third party hard disk recovery services.

A related opportunity can arise when information is written to an area of a disk storage media that later becomes partially damaged. Such areas are flagged by the operating system as unusable or "bad tracks" and can be difficult or impossible to erase by overwriting techniques.

Information might also still be readable in the event of a failure in a part of the media or a corruption of the FAT. A special utility program might be used to copy a file where one or more of the sectors are no longer readable due to a failure in the disk media. Files may also still be intact even though the FAT is corrupted.[19] In such a case, a disk editor might be used to search and recover the individual blocks of the desired file. It may also be possible to use a program such as PowerQuest's *Lost and Found* to repair and restore the damaged disk.

Note: When recovering deleted files (i) exercise care so that any active file with the same name is not erased; (ii) immediately move any undeleted file to a different storage device; and (iii) undelete files only one by one so that other recovered files with the same name are not overwritten.

(c) Data Remanence

Even when the information on magnetic storage media has been deleted and the space re-used to store new information, or even overwritten with useless data through the use of a "WIPE" utility program such that it cannot be recovered using ordinary system capabilities, it may still be possible to read old information by using special-purpose hardware and special laboratory techniques. The effectiveness of such techniques is increased when the magnetic media has been stored for

---

18 For an example of a program that can be used to view such data, see *Directory Snoop* from Briggs Software.

19 Note that some utility software programs periodically update a second backup copy of the FAT that can be accessed in the event the primary copy is corrupted.

either an extended period of time or at high temperature conditions (120 degrees Fahrenheit or greater); or where there has been equipment failure or mechanical faults, such as misalignment of read/write heads. In some cases this will yield a weak but still readable magnetic trace from the older information. This is the reason that the US Government standards for erasing information require re-writing to the same spot multiple times.[20]

For more information, see The National Computer Security Center's "A Guide to Understanding Data Remanence in Automated Information Systems."[21]

4.3 PRINT SPOOLERS

Most computer systems are capable of processing a print operation faster than the attached printer can actually output the printed pages. This led to the popularity of programs known as print spoolers. Print spoolers capture a print job from any software application program and store it as a temporary file on the disk so that the application program will think that the printing was complete and could go on to perform other work. The print spooler will then operate in the background and feed the print job to the printer at the printer's required pace.

Originally, print spoolers were sold as add-on programs for *MS-DOS* users. With the advent of Microsoft *Windows*, this feature was added to the operating system and is known as the "print manager". The print manager stores each print job as a temporary file that is deleted when the printer has completed printing that particular print job. It may be possible to search for deleted files used by the print manager where the disk space has not yet been re-allocated to a new file. These deleted files, if recoverable, can be used to re-create a prior print job or at least identify what has been printed.

Some older systems may utilize a print spooler contained in an external hardware device that is connected between the computer and the printer. These devices may potentially contain a print job if the printer was not ready when the print command was given. Some laser printers may also contain an internal hard disk that is used to store an image before it prints. Such information will stay on the hard disk until it is overwritten.

---

20 Government standards usually require alternatively overwriting with 1-bits and 0-bits three times and then overwriting with a value of F6h. A final pass is also made to verify the F6h write.

21 NCSC-TG-025. See <http://biblio.isu.edu/security/isl/drinais.html>.

4.4 MICROSOFT *WINDOWS* DESKTOP OPERATING SYSTEM

(a) The Swap File

Microsoft's *Windows* operating system has become one of the most popular operating systems on the desktop. One of the characteristics of *Windows* is that it utilizes a normally hidden file called the "swap file" as a large temporary data buffer to run programs and load data files that do not fit into available random access memory (RAM). An analysis of the swap file using special utility programs (see Appendix) may reveal fragments of documents, Internet URLs, network passwords and other useful information.

(b) The *Windows* Registry

32 bit versions of *Windows* (*i.e.*, *Windows 95* and above) utilize a database called the "Registry" to track information about hardware, software and user preferences. The Registry has been described as "the heart of *Windows*" (particularly, starting with *Windows 98*). In a typical work session, the Registry may be assessed tens of thousands of times by the operating system and the application programs utilized during that session. Information stored in the Registry may, therefore, provide valuable evidence of various activities conducted on the PC.[22]

In earlier versions of *Windows* (*Windows 3.x*), most hardware and software settings are saved by text files having the extension "INI". The primary INI files used by *Windows 3.x* are WIN.INI, SYSTEM.INI, CONTROL.INI and FROGMAN.INI. Individual application programs may also store information in private INI files located in the "WINDOWS" or "WINDOWS\SYSTEM" directories or in the directory where the application is installed. With *Windows 95* and above, much of the information formerly contained in these INI files has been consolidated in the Registry along with additional information pertaining to new features incorporated into the later versions of *Windows*.[23]

With *Windows 98*, the Registry primarily consists of two hidden files "user.dat" and "system.dat", both stored in the "C:\WINDOWS" directory (although some limited information may also be stored in WIN.INI and SYSTEM. INI, also found in the "C:\WINDOWS" directory). In addition to the active copy of the Registry,

---

22 Software documentation accompanying *Windows* contains little information about the Registry. However, a good overview for our purposes is contained in *Windows 98 Registry for Dummies*, by G.E. Weadock & M.B. Wilkins (Foster City, California: IDG Books, 1998).

23 Some of these files may continue to exist on older PCs which have been updated to newer versions of *Windows*.

multiple backup copies may also be present on the PC (not to mention backup copies of the hard disk).

Windows 98 automatically creates a backup copy of the Registry the first time the PC is turned on each day (in contrast to *Windows 95*, that saved a backup copy each time the PC was turned on even if this was done multiple times in the same day). These automatic backups of the Registry (that includes the key Registry files of the default user plus WIN.INI and SYSTEM.INI) are stored in a compressed filed called RB0xx.CAB in the directory "C:/WINDOWS/SYSBCKUP", where "xx" is a sequence number that can range from 00 to 99.

Note that SYSBCKUP is a hidden folder that may not be visible unless Windows is configured to display hidden files and directories. By default, Windows 98 saves the last five backups (although advanced users may change this setting).

The user of the PC may also have created backup copies of the Registry, from time to time, using tools provided in *Windows*, such as *Registry Checker*, or using third party tools. Third party registry backup programs may create copies of the Registry that have names such as SYSTEM.NUx and USER.NUx, SYSTEM.NAV and USER.NAV, and SYSTEM.PCA and USER.PCA.

Some PCs are set up with multiple user profiles so different users can log on to the same PC and use their own settings and defaults. On PCs where multiple user profiles have been enabled, the USER.DAT file associated with a particular user can store application program settings. As well, the "C:\WINDOWS\PRO-FILES*USERNAME*" directory may contain the following files or folders:

- Application Data—Outlook Express address book and indexes;
- Cookies—Internet Explorer cookies—files that contain information accessed by some Web sites;
- History—Internet Explorer history information—Web addresses of recently visited sites;
- Temporary Internet Files—Used by Internet Explorer to store copies of recently visited Web sites;
- Favorites—Used by Internet Explorer to store favourite places;
- Desktop—Stores desktop icons and folders;
- Recent—List of recently opened documents;
- Nethood—Shortcuts added to the Network Neighbourhood folder;
- My Documents—Folder to store documents; or
- Start Menu—Shortcuts added to the default start menu.

Windows 95 stores individual profile copies of USER.DAT and SYSTEM.DAT (along with backup copies) in "C:\WINDOWS\PROFILES\USERNAME" (with the single backup copy having a DA0 extension). As previously described, USER.DAT contains user-specific information (such as recently used file lists). The SYSTEM.DAT file contains hardware configuration data and information about installed software (but not settings for individual users). These files may contain evidence that certain software was installed or used in the past or of certain activity conducted on that PC.

It should be noted that *Windows* supports a function called "Remote Registry" which is a network service that facilitates central administration of the Registry files contained on networked PCs. This is another reason to disconnect any network connected PC where the preservation of electronic evidence is desirable.

(c) The GUID and Microsoft Office Products

Another source of useful information contained in files created using Microsoft Office products (*Word, Excel, PowerPoint* and possibly *MS Access*) is an identifier linking the file to the particular computer that was used to create the file.

Personal computers are connected to local area networks by means of a network interface card (NIC) that typically takes the form of an expansion card that is inserted into desktop computers. Each NIC contains a unique identifier or "address" (essentially, an electronic serial number).

When *Windows 98* is installed on a PC containing a NIC, its address is copied to the Windows Registry (a special file used to track configuration information). A unique number is generated internally for any *Windows* PC without a NIC. In either case, this identification number is labelled in the Registry as the Global Unique Identifier (GUID).

Microsoft Office products (including its Microsoft *Word* wordprocessor, *Excel* spreadsheet and *PowerPoint* presentation software) embed the GUID of the PC used to create the document into each document created on that PC. This apparently also occurs in *Windows 95*. The result is a digital fingerprint that can be used to match a document with the computer on which it was created.

A special type of program known as a binary editor must be used to view special format codes embedded in Microsoft Office documents, including GUID.[24] However, more user friendly utility programs may also be available to find and display such information.

The electronic registration process used by customers to register their copy of *Windows* (in order to qualify for support and updates) transmits the GUID to Microsoft as part of the registration information that generally includes the user's name, address, phone number, demographic information, and technical details

---

24 Search for GUID towards the end of the document.

about the user's system. The result is a database that can allow Microsoft to match a NIC identifier to a particular PC owner.

After enduring harsh criticism from privacy advocates in the Spring of 1999, Microsoft indicated that it would purge such information from its internal databases and that it would alter the way the registration process works in the maintenance release of *Windows 98*. However, there are no indications that any changes will be made to any of its Office products and these products will likely continue, by default, to embed the GUID into each document they produce. It should, however, be noted that Microsoft released tools which allow a user to delete the GUID from a particular file.

In late March 1999, a malicious *Word* virus called Melissa was released on the Internet. Computer experts reportedly used the embedded GUID to trace the Melissa virus back to its creator, David L. Smith, who was arrested April 2, 1999.

4.5 HARD DISK PARTITIONS

Hard disks should be examined using a program like *FDISK* (that comes with *DOS* or *Windows*) or comparable utility software to ascertain whether hidden partitions may have been created. Such partitions may normally be invisible to the operating system in use on the target computer and may require use of special utility programs to gain access.

4.6 NETWORK OPERATING SYSTEMS AND FILE SERVERS

A network operating system is the operating system that runs on network file servers attached to local area networks. Most network operating systems have features similar to those found in desktop operating systems such as *MS-DOS* or *Windows*.[25] The following discussion will focus on features found in *Netware,* one of the more popular network operating systems. Similar features may also be incorporated in competitive systems.

Files deleted from a network file server, like those deleted from a workstation's hard disks, are normally recoverable. It may even be easier to recover a file deleted

---

25 Popular high-end network operating systems based on a dedicated server design include Novell's *Netware*, Banyan's *Vines*, IBM's *OS/2 LAN Server* and Microsoft's *Windows NT*. The other type of network operating system, known as a peer-to-peer network, does not incorporate a dedicated file server. Examples include Microsoft's *Windows for Workgroups* and Artisoft's *Lantastic*. Computers running *Windows 95* and *Windows 98* can also be connected together as a peer-to-peer network.

from a file server than a local workstation. *Netware*, for example, places the space occupied by deleted files into a special first-in first-out queue so that the recovery of deleted files can be more predictable. In addition, it is capable of tracking and retaining multiple deletions of different versions of the same file.

In *Netware*, a special utility called SALVAGE is used to access a list of the most recently deleted files and to perform the recovery operation. The network operating system tracks a number of different attributes about each deleted file. The list of deleted files can be sorted according to various file attributes in order to facilitate the search for a specific deleted file.[26]

Another related *Netware* utility called PURGE is used to erase permanently copies of any recoverable deleted files that are accessible to a particular user. A file server administrator can request an erasure of all files located on the file server. The PURGE utility performs the same function carried out by a WIPE utility on a local workstation hard disk. Alternatively, a server configuration can be set to purge any deleted file immediately so that recovery is never possible.[27]

Another source of hidden information on a workstation's hard disk discussed previously was information contained in the tail end of re-allocated disk blocks. Network operating systems, unlike their desktop counterparts, were designed for multi-user operations that demand a more secure environment. Consequently, most network operating systems clear out older data contained in re-allocated disk blocks so that confidentiality is not compromised between users.

The print sub-system is another location for potentially useful and hidden information on a network. When a user at a stand-alone computer system sends a print job to an attached printer, the job is sent directly to that printer for processing.[28] However, when a user on a network workstation sends a print job to a network printer, even to a network printer directly attached to that user's workstation, the job is routed to the file server and then delivered to the printer by what is known as a print server.

---

26 Files can be sorted by deletion date/time, file size, filename and by the name of the user who deleted the file.

27 This is accomplished by setting the "Immediate Purge of Deleted Files" setting to "On" in the server AUTOEXEC.NCF file. It is important to check this configuration because if not set to "On" (and the default is "Off"), then the server should contain a large quantity of salvageable files. If it does not, or if only directories other than any relevant directory containing salvageable files, then this may indicate that a PURGE function may have been run on the entire volume or on the relevant directory. Also, when reviewing salvageable files present on a particular volume, it is useful to review how far back in time the oldest salvageable files are from (once again, to help assess whether any tampering has occurred).

28 The print job might, however, be intercepted by a print spooler program or *Windows* Print Manager program as discussed previously.

When a print job leaves a network workstation, it is stored temporarily in a print queue on the file server.[29] The queue holds the job until the print server can deliver it to the appropriate printer. When the printer is ready to print the next job, the print server sends it from the queue to the printer. After a print job has been successfully printed, it is deleted from the print queue.

If, however, a printer is turned off, has an out-of-paper condition or, for some reason, is not functioning properly, then a print job will remain in the print queue and might be captured as part of a periodic system backup. Also, to the extent that the disk space utilized by a completed print job has not been re-used, it may be possible to use the SALVAGE command to recover the contents of a particular print job.

Network file servers may also be running an accounting process to "charge" users for disk space, file server utilization, or other network resources. If this option is active then it may provide audit logs of certain types of user activity. In addition, some sites use third party security utilities that can provide a comprehensive audit trail of what people did while they were on the system.[30]

In the case of files stored on shared network file servers, it would be useful to ascertain the access control records or lists for the sub-directory or folder where the relevant evidence was contained. This would provide information as to which individuals might have had access to manipulate such files.

4.7 BACKUP TAPES

Information stored in a computer system can be lost due to an inadvertent erasure or computer malfunction. As well, databases can become corrupted.[31] Consequently, a copy of the information stored on the hard disk of most computer systems

---

29 On a server using *Netware* software, each print queue has its own sub-directory that is created under the SYSTEM sub-directory on the SYS volume (by default). Each individual print job is stored as a distinct file under the appropriate print queue sub-directory.

30 *I.e.*, what programs were run, what files were created, deleted or modified, etc.

31 Corruption of a database may mean that access to some of the records will be lost or that access to the entire database is affected. If the corruption only occurs in the index files than a re-building of such index files by the computer may solve the problem. If the corruption is more serious or has affected the file housing the actual database records, then a backup copy of that database will need to be restored from a backup tape.

In some cases, database corruption may not be immediately evident. It may not be discovered until a user experiences a problem searching for a record he or she knows should be in the database. For this reason, many backup strategies retain backup tapes for a longer period of time then would seem necessary, in order to perform a restore of the system in the event of a malfunction.

is usually backed up periodically on magnetic tape. Most organizations have a formalized procedure to ensure that such backups are made frequently and at regular intervals.

The most common methodology applied is to make a full backup of the entire system on a daily basis. Alternatively, a full backup is made once a week, or every other day, with a smaller backup of all files modified since the last full backup, being made on days when a full backup is not performed. Multiple tapes are commonly employed as part of a "backup cycle".

A common backup strategy is to use a separate backup tape for each day of the week except Friday (although this can be any designated day of the week). The "Monday" tape is re-used the following Monday and so on. A separate backup tape is set aside and used for each Friday of the month (e.g., Friday 1, Friday 2, etc.). The backup tape utilized for the first Friday of each month is re-used the first Friday of the following month. Each time a tape is re-used, the older information on that tape is overwritten and destroyed.[32] An organization utilizing such a backup strategy would be able to restore lost information that was copied to a tape from as long as one month earlier.[33]

In addition to the above procedure, some organizations also use a new backup tape for one designated day of each month (e.g., first Friday of each month) and then put this tape aside for permanent retention. In such a case, it may be possible to retrieve data that was deleted anytime in the past.[34] However, any information created and then deleted on the same day (and before the backup was performed) would not be captured on any backup set.

Due to the growing volume of computer-readable data many organizations are finding that these traditional backup techniques are no longer sufficient to allow an entire backup to fit on a manageable number of tapes or to take place entirely during non-business hours. Many sites are exploring the use of new backup technologies, including what is known as hierarchical storage management (HSM) systems, that promise faster backups and near bottomless pits of storage.[35]

---

32 Unless of course, the information most recently recorded is smaller in size than the information previously recorded on that tape. In which case, portions of older backups may still be recoverable.

33 Assuming the information was retained long enough on the system to be captured on one of the weekly backup sets. In other words, it existed on the system on the day that a weekly backup tape was used and, therefore, retained until that tape was re-used the corresponding week during the next month.

34 Assuming the information was retained on the system long enough to be recorded on one of these monthly backup days.

35 HSM systems automatically move files between more expensive higher-speed magnetic disk drives and less costly, but slower jukebox-based optical disks and magnetic tape units. The underlying concept is to create a multi-tiered system that dynamically moves infrequently accessed data to lower levels, where it resides on less expensive storage

In some implementations of HSM, a placeholder remains on the primary disk when a file is migrated to HSM storage. This placeholder is used when a user requests a directory of files or certain system information about a file. A deletion of a file initially may delete only the placeholder rather than the real file on the HSM system. Also, since the lower levels of HSM storage[36] cannot randomly erase files, such systems may retain copies of supposedly deleted files for a long period of time.

To protect against catastrophes such as fire, flood and earthquakes, many organizations move some or all of their backup tapes to an off-site location for storage. Such tapes are typically sent by special courier on a daily or weekly basis, with older tapes being returned in time for re-use in the backup cycle.

In addition to these formalized regular backups, an organization may also have backups that were made on an *ad hoc* basis or in response to a certain event. For instance, it is not uncommon for system operators, or other support staff, to make an *ad hoc* backup prior to installation of new software, a software upgrade, or a hardware upgrade.

Many individual users may also make their own personal backups of their own work (typically on floppy diskettes). Such backups may be made to serve as a permanent archive of documents that no longer need to be retained on the system, or as a way to transport a copy of work-in-progress between the office computer and a laptop or home computer.

Magnetic tapes used to store backups share a similar ability to retain old information. Information is usually recorded to magnetic tapes starting at the beginning of the tape. Like audio and videotapes, if the newer information recorded on top of the older information is shorter than the older information, then a portion of the older information will remain at the end of the tape.

This can be analogous to a VCR tape containing two half-hour television programs that is then re-used to store a 20-minute news clip. The re-used tape will still contain the last 10 minutes of the first program and the second program in its entirety. Standard tape duplication software does not copy these remnants of older information. Putting older backup tapes aside is, therefore, preferable if the information they contain must be preserved for litigation-related purposes.

---

media. Medium speed, randomly-accessible erasable media, such as re-writeable optical disks serve as a secondary level of HSM storage to hold files most likely to be needed by users (next to those required all the time that are stored on the hard disk that forms the primary level). Lower-speed media that cannot be erased randomly, like tape or write-once optical disks, provide a tertiary level of HSM storage where little-used files can reside.

36 For example, information stored on tapes or once-write optical media.

Finally, each time a backup process is run, an entry is commonly made to a log file that contains the date and time of the backup along with a description of the information that was backed up. This log file is typically cleared or reset periodically. It may or may not be backed up to tape along with the other files contained on a computer system. An examination of this log file can reveal the existence of backup sets that were made but may not have been disclosed.

4.8 DATABASES

Databases are used to store all sorts of business and personal information. A database can contain one or more tables. For example, an accounts receivable database may contain a table with a listing of all of the business's customers. Another table could contain all of the invoices. Other tables might be look-up or validation tables such as a list of all of the provinces. Some databases store multiple tables in the same database file while others utilize a separate file to store each table.

Within each *table* are multiple records. Each *record* contains information about one basic item. For example, each record in a customer table would contain the information about one particular customer. The information about each item (*e.g.*, customer) is contained in one or more *fields*. Each record contains the same number of fields (although information might not be entered into each field). The number of records in a table, however, does not stay constant but increases as new items are added or decreases as items are removed.

Records are typically stored in a table sequentially as they are added. If it is desirable to view the records in a different order (for example, sorted by customer name) then one or more indexes are created. The physical arrangement of each record is not usually changed but rather the index is consulted whenever a user wishes to view a database in a particular order. These indexes may be stored in the same database file as the tables, or may be stored in its own separate disk file depending on the database.

If a record in a database is deleted, then that record is flagged as "deleted" and will stop appearing during most database operations. However, the information contained in that record is not actually erased. With some databases, new records added to the database utilize the space occupied by these deleted records while in other databases the new records are added to the end of the file.

In order to erase the information contained in these deleted records permanently, a special procedure sometimes called "packing" or "compressing" the database must be run. In some cases this is accomplished through a re-write of the active database records to a new database file and a deletion of the old database file that contained the "deleted" records.

The procedure to actually erase the deleted information and reclaim the space it occupied is usually not run very often. The result is that deleted information may continue to exist for weeks, months, or in some cases, years after its apparent deletion. In addition, an examination of the computer system shortly after a database compression operation may still yield the older version of the database in the form of a deleted disk file whose space may not have yet been re-allocated to a new file.

Another useful source of information about databases can be obtained by an examination of transaction files created by certain types of database management system known as client/server systems. This type of database system was designed with certain safeguards to reduce the risk of data loss in the event of computer failure. All transactions (*e.g.*, additions, deletions or modifications) processed by this type of database are recorded in a sequential transaction log.[37]

In the event that a computer failure causes a corruption in the database, an older copy of the database can be loaded from the last system backup and then the transactions contained in the transaction log can be processed to bring the database back to its current state. An examination of this transaction log, recorded during the desired period, can be used to reconstruct what took place.[38]

4.9 WORD PROCESSING FILES

Word processing files contain numerous examples of electronic information not typically found in the printed copy of a document. These include:

- Document summary fields—These are optional fields that can be used to store information about a document.[39] Some organizations that do not utilize a document management system can make extensive use of this feature to store information about the documents they generate;
- Comments—Users will sometimes want to comment on a document but not change the content. A comment or annotation feature allows a user to select the text to be commented on and then opens a separate annotation pane where the comments are typed. Comments made by different people may be tracked

---

37 This transaction log is typically cleared or reset each time the database is successfully backed up to tape.

38 A copy of the relevant transaction log would have been recorded on the system backup tape for the relevant time period.

39 *WordPerfect* and Microsoft *Word* both provide default fields that can be used to store information about the document. *WordPerfect* automatically fills in the creation date, author and typist of a document. Microsoft *Word* may capture the author, the date the document was created, last saved, who last saved the document, a revision number, total editing time spent in the document and the date and time the document was last printed. Similar information is captured and stored in other Microsoft applications such as Microsoft *Project* and *PowerPoint*.

and shown separately. With appropriate hardware, comments can include a voice and pen annotations as well as text. Pen annotations can be added directly to the document and are treated like any other drawing object. Comments are normally hidden from normal view unless the feature to view comments is turned on. Comments will not normally print with the document unless specific print settings to print the comments are turned on;[40]

- Revision Tracking—A "revision marking" function can be used to track changes that are made to a document. Revision marks can show where, when and by whom changes have been made in a document. If several people revised the same document, Microsoft *Word* can assign a different colour to each reviewer's marks and label each revision with the reviewer's name and date/time of the revision. Revision marks can be added while the document is being edited. Depending on the settings, the revision marks can be kept hidden, shown only on screen and/or shown on printed copies of a document;
- Dictionaries—Dictionaries may contain the names (of individuals, product names or companies) used in correspondence or other documents even after the relevant documents have been deleted. *WordPerfect* provides two types of dictionaries that can be searched—a "supplemental user dictionary"[41] and a "document dictionary"[42] Microsoft *Word* allows the creation of one or more custom dictionaries for this purpose;
- Hidden text—A feature referred to as "hidden text" allows a user to insert into a document text that will not appear on the screen or printed copy unless special action is taken;
- Tables—Tables in word processed documents are like small spreadsheets. As such, access to the electronic copy of a document can provide access to formulae that may have been inserted in cells but which will not appear in the printed version;
- Suppressed headers and footers—The information contained on headers or footers can commonly be suppressed from appearing on the screen or printed version of a document by inserting a special "suppress code"; and
- Undo—Information concerning recent changes to the document (including deletions) may be retained within the document in order to support the use of an UNDO feature. *WordPerfect* 8.0 can store up to 300 actions in its UNDO buffer (although the default is 10 and a configuration option is available to prevent the UNDO actions from being stored in the document).

---

40 Microsoft *Word* supports the use of annotations in the hidden text section. The initials of the annotation's author are typically recorded along with the annotation. Like hidden text, the existence of annotations, and their content, may not appear when the document is printed or displayed on the screen unless special commands are given.

41 A supplementary dictionary is created for each user and used to add words or names to be skipped if found in any document being spell-checked by that user.

42 A document dictionary is a mini-dictionary incorporated into the actual document. A document dictionary is useful if there are words or names to be skipped for a particular document only or if multiple people will be editing the same document.

Other types of information may be captured or tracked by a word processing program but not necessarily stored within a particular document. Such information is typically tracked separately in respect of each user of the program and may include:

- Address books—An address book facility may be available to store the addresses of people and organizations. The information may be collected and stored when certain word processing templates are utilized in order to provide quick access to these same addresses at a future date for faxing, or addressing letters or envelopes. The information contained in the address book is typically saved in special configuration or data files;
- Search and Replace—Many programs store the last few entries that were searched for by a particular user;
- Log files—Certain versions of *WordPerfect* support the creation of optional log files that can contain an audit trail of the names of all documents that have been edited;
- Last opened file names—Many *Windows*-based programs now retain a list of the last few documents that were edited by a particular user.[43] The START MENU, introduced in *Windows 95*, has a "Documents" selection which tracks the last 15 documents (word processing and other types of documents) that were accessed by certain programs;[44] or
- Indexer—*WordPerfect* incorporates a built-in file indexer that can be used to create a searchable index of the full-text of all documents located in a specified directory. These indexes are only updated periodically. A search of such indexes using keywords related to a litigation matter or investigation may reveal the existence of a relevant file that was deleted since the last time the index was updated.[45]

Many word processing programs also contain a number of otherwise hidden sources of information that, in some cases, can be retrieved with expert assistance. These may include:

- Fast save—This is a feature that can be used to speed up the time it takes to save a copy of the current document to disk. The improvement in speed comes from the fact that only incremental changes are saved (*i.e.*, the parts of the document that have been added, replaced or marked for deletion). Intermediary

---

43 For example, *WordPerfect* 6.1 retains a list of the last 10 documents that were accessed by a particular user. By default, *Word97* displays the last four files that were worked on. However, a configuration setting can be changed so that *Word97* displays the last nine files.

44 However, the tracking by *Windows* of the last 15 documents can be disabled using the *Windows' TWEAK UI* applet (Paranoia tab).

45 A file that existed at the time the indexer was last run but has since been deleted would show up in a key word search of the index even if the actual file can no longer be retrieved.

changes, including sections of the text that were deleted, may actually be recoverable;[46]

- Retention of previous version[47]—This is an option that forces the retention of one previous version of all documents. The older version is renamed with a particular extension[48] and retained in the same sub-directory as the newer version. Some minicomputer operating systems, such as VMS, may be set to do this automatically.[49]

- Method of saving new versions—This may involve renaming the older version of a file followed by a rewrite of a new file each time the document is saved. With *WordPerfect*, the older version is renamed with a "bk!" extension, the document is written out to the original file name, and then, if the "Original Document Backup" feature is not turned on, the older version is deleted. This provides protection in the event the computer malfunctions during the save process but can result in numerous older versions of a document remaining on the disk in a deleted but recoverable state;

- Extensive use of temporary files—If a very large document is retrieved into a word processing program then a portion, that can be almost as large as the entire document, may be written out to one or two temporary files to speed a "GOTO" operation to the start or end of the document. Temporary files may also be utilized to store a copy of text deleted from the document in order to support the undelete feature in the software;

- Timed document backups—A timed backup feature may cause a copy of the document being edited to be written to the disk periodically. This type of facility is used to allow a user to partially restore his or her work in the event of a power failure or other problem. This timed backup copy is deleted when the user exits the word processing program. It serves the purpose of allowing the user to recover a document that was not saved, as it was at the last timed backup, in the event the computer should malfunction.[50] Each time a timed backup copy is saved, typically between five and 15 minutes, the older copy is renamed and deleted. All these deleted timed document backup copies may be in a deleted file but still recoverable state on the storage media;

- Invisible headers—Some word processing programs save certain system information to the header of each document file. This information is not generally accessible by a user through the normal operation of the word processing program. However, it may be viewable using special utility software; or

---

46 This function is present in both *WordPerfect* and *Word* and by default is enabled.

47 Called "Original Document Backup" in *WordPerfect*. A similar feature is available in Microsoft *Word* by checking the "Always create a backup copy" selection under "Save options".

48 In the case of *WordPerfect*, the older version of a file is saved with a "bk!" extension.

49 For instance, VMS may be programmed to keep the original version and three prior versions of each document. The older versions would have a 1, 2 or 3 suffix appended at the end of the file name.

50 If the word processing program is restarted after an abnormal termination, a list of automatically saved documents is presented to the user for recovery.

- Modified save function—Some organizations modify their word processor software installations so that the program will run a special macro each time a document is to be saved. For instance, a backup copy of any document being saved may be copied to the user's local hard disk so that it can be accessed in the event of a network failure. It is, therefore, important to ask questions regarding whether the particular installation of any relevant software has been modified or enhanced in any way, particularly in respect of the save function.

While the information and techniques contained in this section were written in reference to word processing documents, many of these features and potentially hidden sources of useful information may also be applicable to other software programs including spreadsheet[51] or presentation graphics programs.

It should be noted that a number of programs written for *Windows* support a "linking and embedding" function that allows a user to insert an "object" from another application into a document. Macintosh computers contain a similar feature called "publish and subscribe". Using this feature, a user can attach a graph or spreadsheet created by a spreadsheet program onto a letter created by a word processing program. The external object will appear within the document. However, depending on the method of attachment, the object may continue to exist outside of the document. Therefore, the deletion of the document containing such an object may not result in the deletion of the object itself.

4.10 E-MAIL

E-mail systems are usually an excellent source of useful evidence for litigation. The shift to the electronic or "paper-less" office is leading to the replacement of office memos with e-mail. E-mail is increasingly used for business communications and copies of messages often seem to be retained longer by the system than expected by its users.

Authors of electronic messages frequently expect that the message will only be seen by the intended recipient and then be deleted. Consequently, they are more likely to make candid comments that would not otherwise be made in formal correspondence.

---

51 For instance, the Lotus 123 spreadsheet program:
   - has facilities to automatically save a copy of a document at preset time intervals;
   - incorporates a version manager facility that can be used to track revisions made by multiple people;
   - contains numerous information about the spreadsheet. The user can enter information for author, title, subject, keywords, comments and revisions. The system tracks information on the date and time the document was created and last revised, the name of the last user to revise a document, the total number of revisions and the total time spent editing a particular document.

E-mail communications may reflect preliminary thoughts or ideas. E-mail messages are not usually reviewed by the organization and typically only reflect the personal opinions of the parties to the communications. However, courts and regulatory authorities may construe these to reflect the organization's position.[52]

Multi-user e-mail systems can be categorized into one of two design types. The first, known as a client/server design, incorporates the use of a program that is utilized by users to communicate with a central e-mail application server that stores and controls access to the messages. The user's program communicates to the e-mail server requests that are then processed under the control of the server. This type of architecture provides greater security and reliability, and allows the server to carry out house-keeping tasks such as automatic enforcement of message retention rules.

The second type of e-mail architecture utilizes a shared directory that is directly accessible to all users and that is used to distribute and store the e-mail messages. Compared to the client/server design, it is not as common for a shared-directory design to have built-in features that can enforce message retention rules.

A common feature found in most e-mail systems is support for folders that can be created by users to store mail messages. Many users use this folder facility to organize copies of e-mail they wish to retain either by topic or by the name of the sender or recipient.

The e-mail system may also create a default folder that is used to automatically store copies of all mail messages sent by that user. The messages stored in this "Sent mail" folder can be deleted periodically by the user on a message by message basis. Users may also be able to specify that a copy of a particular message should not be copied to the "Sent mail" folder.

Another common feature is a facility that allows users to retrieve messages that are deleted accidentally. One method of implementing this feature is to use a system-generated folder to hold copies of all deleted messages.[53] The contents of this folder can be set to flush out when the user shuts down the e-mail program.[54] If the e-mail program for a user is set up to retain deleted messages rather than flushing them out at the end of each e-mail session, then messages may be retained for significant periods of time. If the user is not trained on the e-mail system then he or she may not even be aware that these deleted messages are being accumulated.

The size of each user's e-mail folders will grow as the system is used. Periodically, users may be asked to archive and delete older e-mail messages. A sent-mail folder

---

52 D.S. Skupsky, "The Internet and Business: A Lawyer's Guide to Emerging Legal Issues", Chapter 5, Computer Law Association (1996).

53 In *Microsoft Mail* this folder is called "Wastebasket".

54 *Microsoft Mail* has an option to "Empty Wastebasket when exiting".

is a prime candidate for pruning, because it captures a copy of each message sent out. The archive function will take messages stored in an active folder and "move" them to an external disk file.[55] Therefore, a review of an e-mail system should involve ascertaining whether any archiving was performed, and if so, the location of these files.

In some cases, e-mail folders may be stored on a user's local PC instead of the shared-directory or e-mail database located on the file server. Employees using a laptop or home computer to access a corporate e-mail system will almost always have their folders stored on a remote PC. It is, therefore, important to include these other PCs in a search for electronic data.

E-mail systems may contain additional sources of electronic evidence that can be recovered with expert assistance. E-mail folders and the individual messages they contain, are usually stored in an e-mail file that is a type of database. Mail messages deleted from such a database file are typically not physically removed or erased for performance reasons. Instead, as with other types of databases, the space they occupy in the database file is marked as available for re-use.

Facilities may be available in the e-mail system to purge these deleted messages and recover the disk space being used by such files. However, the purging or compacting facilities are usually only used periodically and usually only when disk space on the drive containing the e-mail files is running out.

Even when e-mail files are purged to recover space, the method used is often one where the entire active (i.e., non-deleted) contents of the file are written out to a new file and then the old file is deleted. The old file may continue to exist on the system in a deleted but recoverable state until the disk space it occupied is required to store new data. Therefore, e-mail information thought to be deleted permanently, may still be recoverable using special utilities to unerase those deleted files.

A high profile example of recovered e-mail occurred during the US Senate's Whitewater inquiry into the handling of Vincent Foster's Whitewater files following his death in 1993. Deleted e-mail messages exchanged between Mr. Foster's secretary and the secretary to then White House counsel, Bernard Nussbaum, were recovered. The messages contained speculation as to whether key evidence in Foster's office had been mishandled by White House officials.[56]

Finally, most large organizations utilize multiple e-mail post offices. Even if all traces of an e-mail message are successfully removed from one post office, it may

---

55 This external disk file can then be taken "off-line" (for example, stored on a floppy diskette) to conserve the more valuable hard disk space. At any time, messages copied to an archive file can be moved back from an archive file to an active folder for review purposes.

56 C. Zehren, *Foster Aide Feared Tampering Newsday* (2 August 1995) A15.

be possible to locate other copies on other post offices if the original message included recipients belonging to such other post offices. Multiple post offices will also be involved when an e-mail is sent from one organization to another. When such communications is sent through the Internet or a third party's network, additional copies may also have been created on intermediate systems.

Some users also utilize more than one e-mail system and each of these should be checked. For instance, some users have an e-mail box on a corporate LAN-based e-mail system, but also utilize a mainframe account or groupware program that provide another e-mail box or e-mail like facility. Many users with home and/or corporate e-mail access may also use one of the growing number of Web-based e-mail services that provides greater flexibility in accessing e-mail and provides greater privacy/anonymity.[57] If users access external databases or on-line services then those may also provide additional e-mail boxes. When searching for e-mail, it is, therefore, important to ascertain all possible locations where e-mail may reside.

In some cases, users with multiple e-mail boxes will configure one or more of these e-mail boxes to automatically forward received messages to a preferred e-mail box so that only one source needs to be checked for new messages. Some of these forwarded e-mail boxes may retain copies of all forwarded messages.

A search for information contained in an e-mail system can be very time consuming. Considering the number of possible backup copies of an e-mail system that may be contained on backup tapes, the review process can become truly expensive. However, such investigations are difficult to avoid when taking into account the potentially incriminating evidence that may exist in such systems.

(a) Novell's Groupwise

One popular e-mail program used in many organizations is *Groupwise* from Novell. *Groupwise* can operate on a shared-directory basis or on a client-server basis.

New e-mail messages are stored in the MAILBOX folder within *Groupwise*. They can be copied or moved to other user-created folders either manually or automatically (through the use of "rules"). Copies of outgoing messages are stored in folder called SENT ITEMS. If an e-mail message is sent to another *Groupwise* user (as opposed to through the Internet) then certain status information may be tracked

---

57 Examples include *Hotmail, Juno, Yahoo Mail, AltaVista, Mail, Net@dress* and *MailExcite*. These types of systems permit employees to retrieve personal Internet e-mail while at work using a Web browser instead of requiring such e-mail to be sent through the company's corporate e-mail system.

(such as the date/time when each recipient "opened" the message, as well as disposition of the message—such as deletion).

Groupwise can be set up to delete or "archive" messages that are older than a specified age. Archived messages are removed from the main message storage facility and stored in a separate archive location where they can continue to be assessed directly from *Groupwise*.

The main system address book (that contains a listing for each user of the system) is called the "Novell Groupwise Address Book". By default, *Groupwise* also creates and opens an address book called "Frequent Contacts" to which e-mail addresses of new recipients (including external recipients accessible through the Internet) are added. The Frequent Contacts address book, therefore, constitutes a sort of log that contains the e-mail address of any person from whom e-mail was received or sent. Any e-mail user can also create additional address books.

Groupwise also permits a version of the program intended for remote use to be installed on a home PC or an office laptop in order to provide remote access. Copies of information erased from the office e-mail system may still be recoverable from such remote and portable systems.

Outgoing e-mail messages are stored in a directory called WPGWSEND, while incoming messages are stored in WPGWRECV. Log files using the template REMOTEx.LOG (where "x" is a single-digit number) store date/time information on connections with the host gateway and logs of file transfers. Additional special purpose sub-directories are used to hold copies of individual e-mail messages and attachments (in a proprietary format). Deleted messages may still be recoverable using unerase tools to recover deleted files that have not yet been overridden with new information.

Updated copies of address books are downloaded upon request from the main e-mail system (and not each time the remote system checks for new mail). This means that even if information about a particular contact person is deleted from the e-mail address book at the office, the information may still be present on a remote client's address book so long as an update of the address book had not been requested since the deletion. Likewise, copies of certain e-mail messages, erased from the office e-mail system, may still be stored on a remote client's e-mail database. Such messages are not restricted to only those that were composed on the remote PC but can include any message that was downloaded to the remote PC for viewing.

It should also be noted that *Groupwise* could also be used to track calendering/scheduling information and to-do lists. Any such information may also be retrieved on an on-demand basis onto remote systems and may be retained on such systems unless specifically removed.

4.11 DESKTOP FAX SOFTWARE

Many office computers have attached modems and are capable of directly sending or receiving faxes. *Windows* comes with a free utility (although limited in functionality) to enable such capabilities. There are also many third party vendors who offer programs with greater functionality. One of the most commonly used such program is *WinFax*.

By default, *WinFax* utilizes four folders:

- OUTBOX—keeps track of faxes in progress;
- RECEIVE LOG—keeps track of in-coming faxes;
- SEND LOG—keeps track of sent faxes (including failed attempts); and
- WASTEBASKET—keeps track of deleted faxes and events (when a fax/event is deleted from one of the other folders, it is moved to this folder—the wastebasket folder may or may not be set up to "empty" when the user exits the program).

The actual copies of the information accessed from these folders are stored in a DATA sub-directory (of the WINFAX program directory). For instance, each page of a received fax is stored as a file with an FXR extension. Each page of a sent fax is stored as a file with an FXD extension. Additional files track information about each event. Even if a particular fax/event is deleted from within the *WinFax* program, it may still be possible to recover unerased copies of the files from the above mentioned DATA directory.

4.12 SOFTWARE SOURCE CODE

"Source code" is a human-readable version of a computer program. In some cases the computer's operation is controlled through the direct execution or interpretation of the source code. However, such handling is commonly very slow. To speed up the procedure, the source code is usually compiled into what is known as machine code or object code that is a form of the computer program that, although not readily understandable by people, is a more optimized form for the computer to run.

As a computer program is developed, the latest version of the source code is continually being saved. Even after a computer program is completed, enhancements and bug fixes are continually made to improve the software. These newer versions of the program are known as upgrades or updates.

In the initial development of a computer program, or as part of the on-going changes made to improve a program, software developers commonly utilize "version control" programs. Such software helps manage the evolution of the software by saving the differential changes between the original version of the software and the on-going changes. Each addition, deletion and modification is tracked.

While a printout of a particular source code file may be identical to the electronic version, multiple electronic versions captured at various phases of its development are more useful in a copyright infringement case where the question of the independent development of the program is in dispute. Such evidence can come from the electronic data contained in a version control system or through the examination of various copies of the source code as it was saved during the development process.

Other sources of the source code in its various phases of development may also be available from third parties such as licensees and/or escrow agents. Certain licensees may have been provided, as part of their licence, with a copy of the source code in order to facilitate their own modification of the software.

Copies of the source code may also have been deposited with an escrow agent or trustee to hold for the benefit of licensees without access to the source code.[58] These copies may also be helpful to a defendant in a copyright infringement action to show independent development by the defendant, or by a plaintiff to show infringing code in a prior version of the defendant's copy of the software.

4.13 WEB BROWSER SOFTWARE

In some cases, employers may wish to review a list of specific Web sites that were accessed by a particular employee.[59] Another purpose may be to address issues related to employee productivity.

Internet activity may be identified by an examination of firewall and proxy server log files and through use of electronic sniffers of network traffic. However, evidence relating to Internet activity may also be identified from data stored on the computer used to access the Internet.

Web browser software programs such as Netscape *Navigator* and Microsoft *Internet Explorer* allow users to "bookmark" sites of interest. The first place to look is, therefore, the bookmark file. Information contained in the bookmark file is retained until deleted.[60]

---

58 Customers may require that a third party hold a copy of the source code so that it can be assured of on-going support in case of the insolvency of the software developer.

59 For example, pornographic sites. Another example may be access to a stock quotation site or an on-line trading system in a case involving an allegation of insider trading.

60 *Internet Explorer* refers to these as "Favorites" and stores each as an individual file in a directory called "Windows/Favorites". *Navigator* stores these in a single file called "bookmark.htm".

Web browsers also typically provide a "URL address" box where a user can directly enter an address of an Internet site. The URL address box may have a "drop-down" button that can show a brief history of Web site addresses that were entered by the user of the browser program.

Web browser programs also create a log of all sites that have been visited using the browser program (including the date and time of the visit). This "history" file retains such information for a period of time that can be configured by a user.[61]

Web browser programs also allow Web sites to upload small pieces of data called "cookies" that are stored in a special file on the user's hard disk. These cookies can be accessed by those Web sites on subsequent visits to associate the latter visit with the previous visit. The "cookie" file can also be reviewed to establish whether a visit was made to a particular Web site (assuming that Web site was one that utilizes such cookies).[62] It should be noted that Web browser programs can be configured to block the creation of cookies and that such information can be deleted by users and/or third party tools which are available to help safeguard privacy on the Internet.

Web browsers also commonly utilize a portion of the user's hard disk to create a "cache" that is used to store copies of recently accessed material. A review of the contents of the cache may provide valuable information regarding the activities conducted on the Internet by a particular user.[63] The amount of space allocated to the cache can be configured by the user. Older files are deleted as new files are added. Users may also manually delete the contents of the cache on an *ad hoc* basis.

Web browser programs may also include e-mail and Usenet news reader components that may contain other information concerning activities conducted on the Internet. Web browser programs may also utilize "plug-in" applications such as Adobe *Acrobat* that may themselves maintain logs of recently accessed documents or other files that make use of the plug-in application.

In some cases, the presence of a particular "helper" application may provide evidence that a particular site may have been visited. For instance, certain adult-oriented sites may require visitors to install unique helper applications in order to receive and display live action video.

---

61 *Navigator* stores this information in a file called "netscape.hst". *Internet Explorer* stores this information in a directory called "Windows/History". The history information is retained for a configured period of time. It may also be cleared manually from time to time.

62 *Navigator* stores this information in a file called "cookies.txt" while *Internet Explorer* uses a directory called "Windows/Cookies".

63 *Navigator* utilizes a directory called "cache" while *Internet Explorer* utilizes a directory called "Windows/Temporary Internet Files".

Many of the above-mentioned sources may also leave copies of deleted files that may still be recoverable. Finally, data remanents of Internet activity may also be present in the *Windows* swap file.

4.14 AMERICA ONLINE SOFTWARE

America Online (AOL) has become the largest on-line service and single organization that connects individual users to the Internet. Special software is required to access America Online, and like many other programs, installation of the America Online software creates tracks of its installation and use.

The installation procedure for version 4.0 of America Online's software creates an INSTALL.LOG file and a VERSION.INF file in the directory in which the program is installed ("c:\America Online 4.0\"), adds an entry to the WIN.INI file and also registers itself with the *Windows* Registry (in numerous locations, including setting the software version, adding uninstall instructions, adding links to permit execution from the Start Menu and a "tray icon").

Many "features" facilitate tracking usage. For example, the AOL software keeps track of the last 25 places visited (History Trail) and supports customization of the toolbar to allow each user to add their own "favorite places".

The America Online directory holds a number of sub-directories, including AOLTEMP (to hold temporary files created by the AOL software), DOWNLOAD (to hold files downloaded from the AOL service), SPOOL and ORGANIZE. A TOOLS sub-directory is used to hold local copies of frequently accessed AOL code. New updates are automatically downloaded on a periodic basis (therefore, an analysis of this directory may provide a rough approximation of when a particular computer last accessed AOL).

America Online permits users to create and use one or more alias (made up usernames that are used on the service to identify the user and protect the user's privacy). The ORGANIZE sub-directory is used to store a file corresponding to each such alias name (the name of each such file is the alias name with no DOS extension), track certain information and defaults corresponding to each such alias name and facilitate logon to the service. A file with the alias name and an extension of ARL is also created to track information about Web sites visited using a particular alias name. Another sub-directory one level down called CACHE is used to hold a cache file corresponding to each alias name. Aside from information contained in such files, the file modification dates may provide information regarding the last date and time a particular user accessed AOL or the AOL software.

AOL also supports a feature called "Automatic AOL" that permits users to perform certain actions off-line (such as reading and responding to e-mail and newsgroup or message board postings). The files stored in the ORGANIZE and CACHE directories mentioned above, among other things, may hold copies of messages composed off-line that are awaiting transmission to AOL. A local address book of potential recipients is also maintained on the PC to facilitate sending of e-mail. Finally, the spell checker used to check messages composed on AOL may contain information about individuals or subjects mentioned in such messages that were not found in the spell checker dictionary.

Of course, the above mentioned information only covers information that is stored locally on the PC used to access AOL. Additional information concerning activity by a particular user is also tracked and stored on the AOL system itself.

4.15 REMOTE CONTROL PROGRAMS

Many corporations and small businesses utilize remote control programs that permit an employee of the company to call in using a remote computer and modem to access their office PC (or a shared PC used for dial-in purposes). Such remote control programs include products such as *ReachOut*, *PCAnywhere*, *Carbon Copy*, *Co-Session* and others. In some cases, employees (particularly those planning to leave) may feel more comfortable making copies of confidential company information using a home computer where they are less likely to be interrupted by other staff.

Many of the remote control programs create log files that may be useful as evidence. The following discussion describes some of the information tracked by one such product, *ReachOut*.

By default, *ReachOut* uses a cache to store frequently used graphics and pictures to reduce the amount of information that must be retransmitted over the remote connection. This is because it is much faster for *ReachOut* to retrieve a copy of such graphics from the local hard disk than to transfer it from the remove computer. The cache file is normally retained (on the hard disk) between sessions in order to make it available for future sessions (cache files have extensions of RCC and are stored in the *ReachOut* program directory). As the cache file fills up, *ReachOut* replaces the least used bitmaps in the cache with the bitmaps most recently retrieved from the remote computer.

ReachOut also maintains an event log with information on all connections and attempted connections to remote computers. The file contains the date and time of each connection, the length of the call, and whether the computer made or received the call (that means that there is a log file both on the computer making the call and the computer receiving the call). Unless turned off, the logging facility also tracks file transfers. By default, *ReachOut* creates or adds to a file named *ReachOut*.RLG in the *ReachOut* directory.

The logging facility can be configured to delete events older than a specified number of days or to overwrite events once the file reaches a specified size. Of course, even when events are deleted, manually or automatically, from the *ReachOut* log file, it may be possible to recover older versions of the file and/or deleted segments of the file.

A caller list can be set up on the PC being called so that calls will only be accepted from callers who can provide an authorized user-ID and password. If activated, this will permit activities to be tracked by particular users (or at least individuals who possess the appropriate user-ID and password information that was provided to a particular user).

4.16 FLOPPY DISK FORENSIC MATCHING

In some cases, it may be useful to show the path used to extract potentially sensitive electronic information. New Technologies, Inc., a developer of forensic software tools for computer evidence processing and the identification of computer security risks, provides tools and training that can be used to match a floppy diskette with the computer that wrote data to it. Although the process is currently tedious and time consuming, work is underway on the development of automated software to assist in the process.[64]

---

64 See <http://www.secure-data.com>.

5

Challenges in Reviewing Electronic Evidence

5.1 DOCUMENT REQUESTS AND PRODUCTION

Document requests need to be specific and unambiguous and need to reference all possible sources of relevant electronic evidence. This includes the various possible locations, computer and backup sources, deleted but recoverable files, end-of-tape segments, etc. The requesting party should be prepared to educate the opposing party, and possibly the court, both of whom may not initially understand the technical issues related to the storage and retrieval of electronic evidence. The same issue regarding educating the opposing party (and their legal counsel) apply in jurisdictions that impose a mandatory obligation on each party to list applicable documents in an affidavit of documents.

5.2 CONFIDENTIALITY

If the discovering party needs to check the electronic source itself, the court may protect the confidentiality of non-discoverable matters and costs of the party being discovered. A protective order can allow disclosure for the lawyer, experts, and/or to selected representatives of the parties only. Where the electronic material contains a mixture of discoverable and non-discoverable information, the disclosing party can inspect the entire program or data and identify the relevant and responsive portions. That party can then object to any portions it identified as not discoverable.

5.3 MAGNITUDE OF INFORMATION IN COMPUTER-READABLE FORM

The magnitude of information stored in electronic form can be enormous. As the price of hard disk storage space has been dropping rapidly, it is becoming increasingly less expensive to retain old information than spend employee time deleting information that is no longer required.

Aside from the potentially damaging impact of information contained in electronic form, the magnitude of such evidence can impose a significant burden if such large quantities of accumulated evidence must be reviewed for the purpose of litigation.

5.4 LACK OF ORGANIZATION

Computer-based information is normally much less organized than its paper-based counterpart. Paper documents are usually stored in indexed file folders, with descriptive tags, and redundant copies are kept in related folders. In many cases, information stored on computer systems is not as well organized, file names may be of a limited size or may not contain descriptive information.

Backup tapes are also commonly not well catalogued. While it may be possible to locate backup tapes made on a certain date, it is usually impossible to identify which tapes contain the backup of a certain file. Even if a sophisticated cataloguing system is utilized to assist in locating individual files, such a system may not be very useful in searching for information captured in backup copies of databases.

5.5 USE OF COMPUTERS TO ASSIST IN THE REVIEW

Each party must examine the materials in its possession or control for relevancy to a particular litigation matter. Relevant materials must then be examined for any privileged information. A party receiving documents produced on discovery must organize the received material, search it for documents useful to the case and then classify the relevant documents according to the issues.

Either party may benefit from the use of a computer to review a large body of computer-based evidence. A computer can be used to locate and group files sharing specified characteristics.[1] A computer can also be used to create a full-text index of all files which can then be searched for specific keywords relevant to the issues.

---

1 Such characteristics may include such things as the date of creation, the user who created the file, a sub-string in the name assigned to the file, etc.

These techniques can be used to narrow the list of possible documents that need to be reviewed by the legal staff.

Some software applications have built-in indexing functions. Many of these, however, only support simple searches for a keyword or groups of words. More sophisticated and specialized search software may be more reliable and efficient at the task. For instance, specialized search software programs may add the ability to use boolean terms, perform proximity searches and support automatic look-ups of synonyms using built-in thesaurus dictionaries.

5.6 REVIEW OF SPECIALIZED TYPES OF DATA

(a) Digitalized Audio-Visual Data

Over the coming years, increasing use of digitalized audio-visual data will likely occur in many business organizations. Many businesses are already using digitalized photographic images incorporated into databases[2] and audio messages that can be routed like e-mail from one voicemail user to another. Video messages may become popular in the future as greater support at the desktop is added for video conferencing. Audio annotations to word processing and spreadsheet documents, referred to as "business audio", is also increasing in popularity.

There will, therefore, be increased intermingling of multimedia with text-based documents on business computer systems. Unlike text-only information, however, the multimedia components cannot automatically be indexed and searched for keywords relevant to the issues of a particular litigation matter.

Instead, the audio or video information needs to be replayed at its recorded speed in order to perform a review for relevancy and privilege.[3] This can substantially increase the already large burden of reviewing such information if a system to categorize the multimedia data is not in place at the time they are created.

---

2 For instance, document imaging programs are being used more and more frequently for document retention and management. Unless such images are converted and indexed, the native image file cannot be searched using automated tools.
3 Audio recordings are not new. There are several organizations that routinely record telephone conversations between their staff and their customers. These include brokerage firms, insurance companies, etc.

(b) Proprietary, Compressed and Encrypted Formats

Many applications store their data in a proprietary file format to conserve disk space and provide quicker access to the data. Information stored in such formats cannot be easily searched using generic search utilities that scan the content of each file on the hard disk looking for specified key words. Unless a special search program can be written to support the proprietary file format used, searching of such files may be limited to the search facilities provided by the specific software.

The use of compression utilities, to reduce the amount of disk space required to store files or programs that are only accessed infrequently, is growing in popularity. A number of related files can also be grouped together into one single compressed file that is easier to handle.

Popular utility programs such as PKWARE, Inc.'s *PKZIP* can substantially reduce the amount of space required by a particular file by looking for patterns in a file and then reducing the size by using compression techniques (*e.g.,* substituting tokens for repetitive data).[4] Some of the compression utilities, *PKZIP* included, also support the use of an optional password to further scramble the data being compressed. Files stored in a compressed format cannot be easily searched and may need to be uncompressed prior to searching.

Several commonly used software programs, including word processing and spreadsheet programs, also support the use of encryption in varying degrees. Some utilize a proprietary encryption format that is useful for protecting the file from casual snooping. However, third party utilities may be available to "break" these less secure forms of password protection. Other programs may use a password to stop a user from directly reading a file using the application that created it but may be easily circumvented by loading the file into a different program.

Some software programs may provide the ability to utilize more secure forms of encryption including the DES[5] or IDEA algorithm. Depending on the length of the encryption key utilized, data protected by these more sophisticated algorithms may be commercially unbreakable.[6]

---

4 This utility creates archive files, called ZIP files, containing one or more files in a compressed state. All attributes of a file, as well as directory structure, can be stored.

5 Data Encryption Standard. A cryptographic algorithm for the protection of unclassified computer data. Promulgated by the US National Institute of Standards and Technology.

6 However, many software vendors choose not to implement very sophisticated forms of encryption so that their products will not be subject to Canadian or US export restrictions that apply to encryption technologies. Others, such as IBM in their *Lotus Notes* product, produce both a North American and an international edition of their product with the international edition incorporating a less sophisticated encryption system.

With respect to document production during discovery, the producing party will likely be required to provide the information in an uncompressed and unencrypted format that can be used by the other party.[7] Where the information is stored in a proprietary format, and where it is being produced in electronic format, then the producing party may be required to produce the information in an industry-standard or open format (*i.e.*, ASCII). Alternatively, the producing party may be required to provide a copy of the appropriate software that can be used to view or print the information.[8] In any case, where information is stored in an encrypted format, the party conducting the discovery will also want to obtain information regarding the encryption software utilized and the identity of all persons who had access to the encryption passwords.

(c) Authentication and Accuracy

Electronic evidence is more susceptible than paper records to corruption, tampering and unauthorized interception. An investigation is, therefore, required of the security procedures and mechanisms that were utilized to protect the integrity of the electronic evidence.

It should be noted that the date and time tracked by *DOS/Windows* can be easily manipulated. Certain third party software programs are even available to help facilitate such manipulation. For instance, see a freeware program called Date Edit from Ninotech Software. In *Alliance and Leicester Building Society v. Ghahremani*,[9] the defendant introduced evidence of a computer printout of a certain directory as evidence of his innocence. The court recognized that "it would be very

---

7 Provincial rules of civil procedure should be amended to create such a requirement explicitly. In the US, Rule 34(a) of the *Federal Rules of Civil Procedure*, provides a definition of documents and also includes a provision that requires the documents to be "translated if necessary, by the respondent through detection devices into reasonably usable form." The Advisory Committee made the following comment on the 1970 Amendment to Rule 34(a):

> The inclusive description of 'documents' is revised to accord with changing technology. It makes it clear that Rule 34 applies to electronic data compilations from which information can be obtained only with the use of detection devices, and that when the data can as a practical matter be made usable by the discovering party only through respondent's devices, respondent may be required to use his devices to translate the data into usable form.

See also, Cal. Civ. Proc. Code §2031(f)(1) that requires the recipient of a document demand, at the reasonable expense of the demanding party, to translate data stored electronically into a reasonably usable form.

8 Note that there may be a licensing problem in doing so. However, consider whether a court order can permit this.

9 [1992] R.V.R. 198 (Eng. Ch. Div.).

simple to reset the computer's clock/calendar for the express purpose of making it appear that a file had been saved to disc on any given date." Other evidence (specifically, the amount of free disk space) cast doubt on the authenticity of the directory printout and it was rejected by the court.

6

Defensive Strategies

A number of defensive strategies can be implemented prior to the commencement of legal proceedings in order to reduce the risk and cost of having to comply with requests for the production of electronic evidence.

6.1 DOCUMENT RETENTION PROGRAMS

(a) Creation of Documents

> In light of increasing discovery of electronic information, a company should encourage employees to draft all documents, especially e-mails, with the expectation that they may be subject to the scrutiny of a judge or jury at some later date in the context of an adversarial proceeding. Sensitize employees through education to the notion that e-mails are not always an appropriate substitute for old-fashioned conversation.[1]

Any company that may have potential liability concerning a particular problem would be well advised to ensure that it does not create an internal record containing expressions of undue alarm. Internal documents should reflect proper concern regarding the problem and the activities being undertaken by the company to address the problem, but should not include an admission of fault or liability. Care should be taken to avoid having persons without appropriate training or skill, or persons who do not have all the relevant facts, making statements of opinions or conclusions. Expressions of concern should be stated in neutral language. Staff should understand that documents may be discoverable in future litigation and should utilize appropriate consideration concerning statements in order to avoid

---

1 Pooley & Shaw, "The Emerging Law of Computer Networks—Finding Out What's There: Technical and Legal Aspects of Discovery" (1996), online: <http://www.fr.com/pubs/paper21.html>.

"smoking guns". Documents should also be drafted in a form that would be easily understood by a judge or jury.

(b) Privilege Issues

Companies should also review what steps should be taken in order to reduce the potential for any incriminating documents being ordered released to another party in future litigation. The best approach is to involve the company's legal counsel throughout the course of any project that may involve potential liability for the company. By being involved in the project on an ongoing basis, counsel may provide guidance as to the circumstances in which the company may wish to assert privilege with respect to certain documents and the steps required to obtain such protection.

Two types of privilege may be applicable to protect the disclosure in legal proceedings (*i.e.*, discovery) of qualifying materials. The first is referred to as legal professional privilege and applies to communications between a lawyer and client for the purpose of the client obtaining legal advice (even if not in contemplation of, or in connection with, litigation). This type of privilege requires:

- that there be written or oral communication passing between a lawyer and one or more client representatives;
- that the communication concern legal advice; and
- that the communication be made in confidence (*i.e.*, that there be no disclosure outside of the lawyer and client relationship).

The second type of privilege allows parties to investigate and assess facts and issues related to litigation or prospective litigation. Litigation privilege protects communications with third parties and is not restricted to communications directly between lawyer and client. To claim litigation privilege:

- litigation must be in progress or must be reasonably anticipated;
- the dominant purpose of the communication must be to obtain advice or to assess or otherwise prepare for litigation; and
- the communication must be made in confidence.

This second type of privilege may be used to protect reports prepared by employees and consultants, provided they are prepared for the purpose of legal advice relating to actual or anticipated litigation.[2] Such reports must be requested by or prepared for the lawyer. Documents prepared in response to requests by management directly to consultants, accountants or risk management advisors will not be accorded the same protection.

---

2 Consultants or other third parties engaged to prepare such reports should be subject to appropriate non-disclosure and other obligations.

Any documentation relating to legal issues, and in particular liability, should be marked as *confidential*, and where appropriate, *privileged*. Access to such documentation should be restricted and should never be distributed to large circulation lists.

(c) Document Destruction

One defensive strategy that can reduce the costs of having to review a large number of electronic documents for relevancy in respect of a production request is to have a well developed document retention program in place. The principle behind a document retention program is that only useful records (that is, records that are relevant and required to deal with business and legal issues faced by the company) should be preserved, and only for the limited period of time during which their retention is useful.[3] A well designed document retention program can be an excellent preventative law tool.[4] It can eliminate the onerous expense of storing of irrelevant and obsolete documents and can reduce the burden and cost of retrieving of documents in response to business requests, government investigations or litigation.[5] Any destruction carried out pursuant to the policy, assuming the policy is otherwise reasonable, should not cause an adverse evidentiary presumption to be drawn. Another equally important purpose is to ensure that relevant and potentially useful records are retained.

What an appropriate retention period is may vary by document category. Some of the issues that should be considered in the selection of an appropriate retention period for each category of document include:

- statutory retention requirements;
- limitation issues; and
- evidentiary issues.

Document destruction that is not based on a reasonable business purpose, but rather is performed for the purpose of frustrating future litigation can harm the company's reputation, result in an adverse evidentiary presumption and provide a basis for

---

3 Parties involved in an action may be required to disclose, at an early stage in the litigation, the categories and locations of electronic evidence that may be relevant to the specific issues raised in an action. It can be a costly and time consuming process to review documents for relevance and possible privilege.

4 R.F. Bianchi, "Document Retention in the Twilight Zone: The Perils of Policies Unpoliced" *Records Management Quarterly* (1 January 1993) at 16.

5 L.H. Guttenplan, "Document Retention and Destruction: Practical, Legal and Ethical Considerations" *Notre Dame Law* 56:5 (1980) 13. See also, P.R. Grady, "Comments: Discovery of Computer Stored Documents and Computer Based Litigation Support Systems: Why Give Up More Than Necessary" *J. Marshall J. Computer & Info. L.* 14:523 (1996).

sanctions or other liability. For instance, in *In re Comair Air Disaster Litigation,*[6] the court concluded that

> the adoption of the 'document management program' in bad faith for the purpose of eliminating unfavorable design and test data from anticipated litigation is sufficient to merit imposition of the severe sanctions. . .

In *Lewy v. Remington Arms Co., Inc.,*[7] the US Court of Appeal had to consider, among other grounds, whether the trial court erred in providing the following instruction to the jury because the plaintiff was unable to produce several documents that were destroyed pursuant to Remington's "record retention policy":

> If a party fails to produce evidence which is under his control and reasonably available to him and not reasonably available to the adverse party, then you may infer that the evidence is unfavorable to the party who could have produced it and did not.[8]

Remington argued that destroying records pursuant to routine procedures does not provide an inference adverse to the party that destroyed the documents. The Court of Appeal was not able to decide, based on the record, whether it was error for the trial court to give this instruction. However, it set out certain factors to be considered on remand if the trial court is called upon again to instruct the jury regarding failure to produce evidence:

> First, the court should determine whether Remington's record retention policy is reasonable considering the facts and circumstances surrounding the relevant documents. For example, the court should determine whether a three year retention policy is reasonable given the particular document. A three year retention policy may be sufficient for documents such as appointment books or telephone messages, but inadequate for documents such as customer complaints. Second, in making this determination the court may also consider whether lawsuits concerning the complaint or related complaints have been filed, the frequency of such complaints, and the magnitude of the complaints.

> Finally, the court should determine whether the document retention policy was instituted in bad faith. . . . In cases where a document retention policy is

---

6   100 F.R.D. 350 (E.D.Ky., 1983). Sanctions were imposed on Piper Aircraft for adopting in bad faith a document retention program which included the routine destruction of flight records and test data sheets if the equipment being tested did not meet minimum standards.

7   836 F.2d 1104, (8th Cir. (Mo.), 1988).

8   Taken from E. Devitt, C. Blakmar & M. Wolfe, 3 *Federal Jury Practice and Instructions* § 72.16 (4th ed. 1987).

instituted in order to limit damaging evidence available to potential plaintiffs, it may be proper to give an instruction similar to the one requested by the Lewys. Similarly, even if the court finds the policy to be reasonable given the nature of the documents subject to the policy, the court may find that under the particular circumstances certain documents should have been retained notwithstanding the policy. For example, if the corporation knew or should have known that the documents would become material at some point in the future then such documents should have been preserved. Thus, a corporation cannot blindly destroy documents and expect to be shielded by a seemingly innocuous document retention policy.

The Court of Appeal also cited the following from *Gumbs v. International Harvester, Inc.:*[9]

[N]o unfavourable inference arises when the circumstances indicate that the document or article in question has been lost or accidentally destroyed, or where the failure to produce it is otherwise properly accounted for.

. . .

Such a presumption or inference arises, however, only when the spoliation or destruction [of evidence] was intentional, and indicates fraud and a desire to suppress the truth, and it does not arise where the destruction was a matter of routine with no fraudulent intent.[10]

(d) Statutory Retention Requirements

Numerous statutes impose record keeping requirements on business entities. Some of these may arise from general laws applicable to all types of business entities, while others may arise from laws that are specific to particular professions or industries. In either case, these requirements are generally applicable to specific categories of records. Examples may include corporate, accounting, taxation and personnel records.

In some cases, such legislation may (i) set out a specific retention period, or (ii) state a minimum retention period in respect of particular types of records. In circumstances where no specific or minimum retention period is specified, the time period for keeping any records should be determined based on the considerations discussed in this section, taking into account that indefinite retention may not be feasible financially.

---

9 718 F.2d 88 (3rd Cir. (Virgin Islands), 1983), at 96.
10 Quoting 29 *Am. Jur.* 2d Evidence §177 (1967).

It should be noted that special obligations to preserve records may apply to certain types of government data. For instance, see subsection 5(1) of the *National Archives Act* (Canada) and the *Federal Records Act* (US).[11] Additional obligations to preserve information may also arise under privacy legislation.

(e) Limitation Issues

Another important consideration that must be taken into account in respect of decisions regarding the destruction of documents is the effect of various limitation periods. Limitation periods are the periods of time during which persons may initiate legal proceedings, as established by the *Statute of Limitations* and miscellaneous other statutes in each jurisdiction. Business records may be relevant to the pursuit or defence of a claim, and accordingly, the types of actions that could be brought and the applicable limitation periods should be considered before records are destroyed. If a business destroys records at the end of a statutory retention period but before the end of a limitation period, it may have destroyed the records it needs to pursue or defend a lawsuit.[12]

Limitation periods vary significantly depending on the type of action and the applicable jurisdiction. The general rule in Ontario is that actions for breach of contract, and torts commonly committed by and against businesses (including negligence), are subject to a six-year limitation period. However, these periods may vary significantly and it is also not always clear when a particular limitation period will commence.[13] For instance, under the Alberta *Limitation Act,*[14] most actions (with a few exceptions) must be commenced no later than two years after the person advancing the claim knew or ought to have known of the claim, or 10 years after the claim arose, whichever period expires first.

A company that operates in multiple jurisdictions will need to design its record retention policy on the basis of the applicable limitation period in each of the jurisdictions where it might be sued, not just the limitation period of the jurisdiction where the records are stored.

---

11 For an example of a case involving the latter, see *Armstrong v. Executive Office of the President*, 810 F.Supp. 335 (D.D.C., 1993), decision affirmed and remanded by *Armstrong v. Executive Office of the President, Office of Admin.*, 1 F.3d 1274 (D.C. Cir., 1993).

12 R.M. Anson-Cartwright, *Records Retention: Law and Practice* (Toronto: Carswell, 1989) at section 1-3.

13 A limitation period typically begins to run when the cause of action accrues. There are three possible times when this can occur: at the time the duty was breached, at the time when all of the essential facts on which the claim was based occurred, or at the "date of discoverability" which can be defined as when the claimant discovered, or ought to have discovered through the exercise of reasonable diligence, the material facts on which the claim is based.

14 S.A. 1996, c. L-15.1.

(f) Evidentiary Issues

Although opinion is divided on the extent to which the destruction of evidence may prejudice a party's case, it is likely that a party that destroys relevant evidence will have an onus to overcome the inference that such evidence contained information prejudicial to the case. The destruction of evidence carries an adverse inference that the evidence destroyed would have been unfavourable to the party who destroyed it, but this adverse inference may be overcome by demonstrating a good reason for the destruction.

According to at least one commentator, the adverse inference or presumption that arises when a party destroys records is likely to be overcome if:[15]

- the party destroyed the records when it was under no legal obligation to retain them (*i.e.*, at the end of any statutory retention period, and where appropriate, after obtaining any necessary permission to destroy them);
- the destruction was performed pursuant to an established document destruction program in accordance with which whole classes of records, rather than selected types of records, were destroyed; and
- any records pertaining to a legal action or anticipated legal action were not destroyed.

(g) Other Design Considerations

The design of a document retention program should take into account certain principles and considerations, including the following:

- Records should be destroyed as a class rather than selectively. Selective destruction may cause negative inferences about their contents to be drawn in any subsequent legal proceedings.
- Destruction of records should be carried out in an orderly manner, based on a predetermined schedule. Should an occasion arise when production of a document is required by law, and the document has been destroyed, it is important to be able to demonstrate that the destruction took place on a scheduled basis, rather than on an *ad hoc* basis.[16]
- Once it is determined that certain types of records are to be destroyed in accordance with an established schedule, the program should extend to multiple copies of a document that may exist (including draft copies). For instance, once an e-mail message or an electronic document is deleted, it would not be

---

15 R.M. Anson-Cartwright, *ibid.*, at section 8-1(1).

16 "Financial Executives Institute of Canada," *Records Retention and Destruction in Canada* (April 1989) at 2.

desirable to retain redundant copies of such documents on backup tapes (except for a short period to guard against system failures).

- The design should include a review of all sources of information, including e-mail and voicemail. Some types of messages may not need to be retained after they are read. For instance, it may be advisable to delete immediately any informal e-mail messages in the same way as voicemail messages are normally deleted after they are heard.
- Consideration should be given to the security measures used to protect electronic data from tampering, alteration, corruption, or destruction.
- The document retention program should also include identification of any personnel that may be unnecessarily saving copies of e-mail messages and other documents that would otherwise have been destroyed through the regular document retention program.
- The document retention program should be implemented as part of a company's normal business and not in anticipation of possible litigation. In fact, the program should incorporate a process to preserve relevant information in the event of litigation or a reasonable likelihood of litigation. It is advisable to isolate or mark such documents in some way to avoid their inadvertent destruction as part of a class of documents in a routine destruction program.
- Legal counsel should be able to override the operation of the document management program when a lawsuit is filed against the company or where it appears likely that one will be filed. A current list of contacts to notify in the business operations area should be maintained for this purpose.
- The document retention policy should include a process for periodic review by legal counsel so that changes in case law and/or statutory requirements can be incorporated. The policy should also be revised if a certain category of documents have been the subject of repeated non-frivolous complaints by customers or other third parties.[17]
- Some companies require their employees to acknowledge compliance with the company's document retention policy as part of those employees' annual agreement to the company's ethics statement. Compliance with the company's document retention program may also be incorporated into the company's internal audit program.[18]

As a general rule, the company should exercise a high level of prudence in deciding what types of documents should be destroyed. Many types of documents related to activities undertaken to address problems faced by the company may be useful to show that the company exercised appropriate diligence and to show the basis upon which decisions were made and actions taken. Aside from use to defend a civil action, such documentation may also be required to substantiate statements that are made (or not made) in respect of disclosure obligations arising from securities legislation. Furthermore, detailed records of documents and correspondence may be particularly important in respect of the work that is being performed by third

---

17 I.C. Ballon, "How Companies Can Reduce the Costs and Risks Associated with Electronic Discovery", *Computer Law* 15:7 (July 1998) 8.

18 DuPont is an example.

party consultants, in the event that such parties fail to complete their obligations in a timely manner or they provide results that are deficient. In such event, the company may wish to assert claims against such parties, or show that any failure or default by the company was the result of the acts of such third party on whom the company was reasonably entitled to rely rather than the result of any default or failure by the company.

(h) Draft Versions

An important issue that should be considered is the action to be taken in respect of draft copies of documents. It is common practice in the preparation of some types of business documents (for instance, a prospectus) to implement a procedure whereby all draft copies of the document are destroyed once the document is finalized.

(i) Selective Backup Strategies

Consideration should also be given to the selection of information to be stored on backup tapes. Instead of making system-wide backups, it may be more desirable, from a preventative risk perspective, to make greater use of selective backup strategies.

In other words, it may be desirable to backup the e-mail system on the daily backup tapes and purposely omit the e-mail database from the weekly backups. In this way, backups are available to restore the e-mail database in the event of a system failure but a backup of the e-mail system is not retained for longer than one week at any one time.

Another benefit of this approach is that it avoids certain problems that may occur if a system based on a single backup of all electronic data is used. In such a system, if the company becomes aware that it must preserve certain information it may need to stop destroying all backups, due to the difficultly (or even impossibility) of preserving selective information from a backup tape while deleting the remaining information on the tape. The net result is that the company will, as a practical matter, lose the ability to destroy certain data that it might otherwise be entitled to destroy.

(j) Additional Information

Additional information on records retention programs may be obtained from the Association of Records Managers and Administrators, Inc. ("ARMA").[19] The following other publications may also contain useful information:

---

19 See <http://www.arma.org/>.

- David O. Stephens and Roderick C. Wallace, "Electronic Records Retention: An Introduction", ISBN: 0-933887-69-8 (ARMA)
- William Saffady, "Managing Electronic Records", ISBN: 0-93387-41-8 (ARMA)
- John T. Phillips, "Organizing and Archiving Files and Records on Microcomputers", ISBN: 0-933887-42-6 (ARMA)
- David Bearman, "Electronic Evidence: Strategies for Managing Records in Contemporary Organizations", ISBN: 1-885626-08-8 (Archives and Museum Informatics)

Oregon State University's *Guidelines for Electronic Records Retention* can be viewed at <http://www.orst.edu/Dept/archives/ARMH/rma63agu.html>.

6.2 SETUP AND CONFIGURATION OF SOFTWARE

Certain setup and configuration changes may reduce the amount of information that is retained concerning particular activities. For instance:

- in the case of word processing programs:
  - turn "fast save" off,
  - turn off the saving of "undo" actions in the word processing document;
- in the case of Web browser software:
  - turn off caching (or reduce the size of the hard disk cache),
  - reduce the length of time a history of activity is retained.

6.3 PERIODIC PURGING OF HARD DISKS AND OTHER MAGNETIC MEDIA

As previously explained, computers do not usually erase deleted information but rather simply mark the storage area previously occupied by the deleted information as available for re-use. The deleted information will gradually be overwritten as the computer system is used to perform routine work.

In some cases this may occur within a few seconds, while in other cases deleted information may continue to exist years after its apparent deletion. In conjunction with the implementation of a document retention program, a procedure should be introduced to purge all remnants of deleted information periodically from computer systems.

The best method for erasing all deleted information from a hard disk or floppy diskette is to utilize a "WIPE" program supplied as part of many PC-based utility software programs. A WIPE program can be instructed to erase completely all information on an entire disk. However, the more typical use would be to erase all disk storage blocks that were in use by deleted files. Such use will erase the deleted files while not harming active files on the disk.

To erase all remnants of deleted files properly, the WIPE program should be configurable also to erase all information contained in the unused portions of the last storage blocks used by active files. This will ensure that any storage blocks belonging to deleted files and re-used as the last storage block by newer files are also erased.

A WIPE program works by purposely overwriting new information on top of all storage locations used by deleted files. Usually the same data (*e.g.*, "10101010" in binary) is written to every location sought to be erased. A disk that exhibits sequential storage locations all containing the same data is an indication that a WIPE program was likely utilized to erase information.[20]

One complication is that some operating systems, including *Windows 95*, cache information written to the hard disk. If the cache is not manually "flushed" after each wipe pass, the dummy data generated by the WIPE program may not be written to the disk if the operating system sees that the file will be erased anyway.

In the case of network file servers, the network operating system can either be configured to purge deleted files immediately, or a PURGE command can be issued periodically in conjunction with the use of a WIPE utility on PC workstations.

End-of-tape information remaining on re-used backup tapes should also be deleted periodically. Many backup software programs contain an ERASE command for this purpose. In addition, a stand-alone magnetic erasure device may be used to erase tapes in bulk.

6.4 ENCRYPTION POLICY

Highly secure encryption of information is becoming easier to perform. Utility software is readily available to encrypt individual files or even entire hard disks. Utility software to perform disk compression[21] or make tape backups also typically allows the user to lock access to the information by using a password. Even common

---

20 As discussed previously, WIPE programs can also usually be configured to overwrite variable data multiple times to each storage location. This may be desirable to reduce the possibility that traces of older information may be read by re-orienting the read/write head of the storage device (a technique that is sometimes used to search for possible faint magnetic traces of the older information that may remain slightly off-centre of the main track used to record magnetic information).

21 For example, Stac Electronic's *Stacker* 4.0.

applications such as word processing, spreadsheet and e-mail programs are now coming with increasingly sophisticated encryption facilities. In many cases, the level of encryption provided by these products is commercially unbreakable.

As the use of encryption becomes more commonplace, many organizations will be increasingly confronted with the problem of producing unencrypted (or "plaintext") copies of electronic evidence that only certain employees with the encryption keys (*i.e.*, passwords) can provide. Increasingly, many employees are being required to remember multiple periodically-changing passwords for authentication purposes. It is not uncommon for employees to forget passwords, especially after a vacation or other break away from the office. When combined with modern labour force mobility, employers may face a growing problem in having to decrypt data when access to the encryption key is no longer available.

It is not known how courts will react to these types of situations. Without access to the encryption key, the party's own counsel will not be able to review the data for relevancy or privilege. Proper disclosure to the opposing party will not be possible. In such situations it can also be difficult to assess whether or not a password was truly forgotten or "forgotten" for convenience.

Even if there is not an absolute obligation to provide unencrypted copies, there may be an obligation to make "best efforts" to do so. This could become very expensive (tracing former employees, employing consultants to attempt to unencrypt, etc.). There is also the problem that information useful to the company may become inaccessible.

Organizations should be advised to implement an organization-wide policy on encryption as part of their risk management strategy. The use of encryption may need to be restricted to a limited number of identified applications. Also, where encryption is used a procedure may dictate that the encryption key be held by more than one employee, or that an encryption system is implemented which supports a key-management protocol where a master-key can be used to override individual keys.

6.5   DOCUMENT MANAGEMENT SYSTEMS

Parties involved in an action may be required to disclose, early on in litigation, the categories and locations of electronic evidence that may be relevant to the specific issues raised in an action.[22] However, most organizations do not have a good idea

---

22   See for example, Rule 30.03 of Ontario's *Rules of Civil Procedure* that sets out the requirement to provide an affidavit of documents to the other party. In Alberta, see Rule 196 of the *Alberta Rules of Court*. In the United States, see s. 26(a) and 16(b) of the new *Federal Rules of Civil Procedure* that went into effect December 1, 1993.

of what information is contained in their computer systems and what has been retained on archival backups.

Without some sort of system to assist in the categorization of documents, the party is placed at risk of not being able to meet its disclosure responsibilities in a timely manner. A failure to disclose in a timely manner can lead to sanctions or to an inference that the party was covering up or had something to hide. Subsequently discovered information that is favourable to a party's position may be at risk of not being admissible into evidence, or may create an impression that it may have been altered or even manufactured.

The use of a document management system will provide assistance in searching for files related to a particular issue. If an effort is made to categorize documents when they are created, the range of documents that need to be reviewed in response to a request for discovery can be reduced significantly by using the facilities of the document management system to identify only the potentially relevant documents. A document management system can also provide greater control over the creation, deletion, modification, viewing and copying of documents.

Courts may not be sympathetic to parties who destroy documents due to inadequate filing systems. For instance, in *U.S. v. ACB Sales & Service, Inc.*,[23] the defendants initially claimed that they could not locate the specific files amongst the millions of files they maintained. They later claimed that some of the relevant files were discarded due to lack of storage space. In refusing to accept the defendant's assertions that the files were destroyed due to lack of space, the court stated:

> . . . a business which generated millions of files cannot frustrate discovery by creating an inadequate filing system so that files cannot be readily located.[24]

6.6 SEGREGATION OF PRIVILEGED FILES

Where a document management system is not utilized, another useful component of a strategy to reduce the costs of complying with a discovery request is to organize the storage of electronic documents so that confidential and privileged documents are segregated. A system should be designed so that, to the extent possible, these documents are being stored in a separate location (folders or sub-directories on the hard disk) and backed up on separate backup tapes. This will assist in the identification of privileged documents, or ones containing proprietary information, and prevent accidental disclosure of the privileged information that was intermingled with other information being disclosed.

---

23 95 F.R.D. 316 (D. Ariz., 1982).

24 Citing *Kozlowski v. Sears, Roebuck & Co.*, 73 F.R.D. 73 (D. Mass., 1976).

6.7 CORPORATE E-MAIL POLICY

(a) Monitoring and Expectations of Privacy

The interception of private communications, whether electronic or otherwise may be prohibited by law. For instance, in Canada, the *Criminal Code*[25] makes it an offence for any person to use a device to wilfully intercept a private communication.[26] Any wilful use or further disclosure of an unauthorized interception may also constitute a separate offence.[27] For the purposes of these provisions, "private communication" is defined to mean "any oral communication or any telecommunication made under circumstances in which it is reasonable for the originator thereof to expect that it will not be intercepted by any person other than the person intended by the originator thereof to receive it".

Certain exceptions[28] are available, such as where the implicit or explicit consent of either the sender or recipient has been obtained. Furthermore, not all types of communications are protected. Transmission logs captured by a computer or telecommunications system may be distinguished from the content of messages and may not constitute "communications". Logging Web sites visited by employees, a feature now routinely provided by most Internet firewall products, may not come within the prohibition of the criminal legislation. Also, an employee's downloading of a Web page does not appear to fit within the above definition of a "private communication".

In the United States, the *Electronic Communications Privacy Act*[29] ("ECPA") prohibits the interception and disclosure of electronic communications. The ECPA permits the owner of a system to inspect or disclose e-mail as a necessary incident to the rendition of service or the protection of the rights or property of the provider of the service. This should permit an employer to inspect and disclose e-mail communications if the inspection is done in the normal course and is necessary for business purposes or to protect that employer's rights or property. However, it is not clear that this exception would permit systematic monitoring of messages that senders would expect to be kept private.

The ECPA also contains an exception where the consent of the originator or intended recipient is obtained. To take advantage of this exception, the employer must announce its monitoring policy prior to actual implementation. Employees who are made aware of the policy and who do not raise any objection may be considered to have given their implied consent to the monitoring.

---

25 R.S.C. 1985, c. C-46.
26 Section 184(1).
27 Section 193.
28 Section 184(2).
29 18 U.S.C. §2701.

Other statutes applicable to electronic eavesdropping or wiretapping may also prohibit an employer from listening in on telephone conversations in which an employee has a reasonable expectation of privacy. However, the applicability of such statutes to e-mail communications is not clear.

Some Canadian provinces have enacted legislation creating a statutory tort for one person to violate the privacy of another. Various federal and state statutes and state constitutions in the United States contain provisions granting citizens explicit privacy rights.[30] Some jurisdictions may also recognize a number of common law torts relating to privacy.[31] One of the key factors that will determine whether an employee may succeed in an action for invasion of privacy is whether the person whose communications are monitored had a reasonable expectation of privacy.

A defensive strategy should include implementation of a corporate policy to govern the use of e-mail and preferably should extend to all use of computer facilities owned by the employer. Such a policy should include an explicit statement that the system is owned by the employer and that messages sent, received or stored by employees on the e-mail system may be reviewed by the employer. The purpose of such a provision would be to reduce or negate an expectation of privacy from being assumed by an employee.[32]

Ideally, the use of e-mail and the operation of the e-mail system should be governed by detailed policies and procedures that can support a position that such messages are generated and retained in the ordinary course of business and should be admissible as business records by the company in any future litigation.

An appropriate e-mail policy will strengthen an employer's ability to utilize such e-mail evidence in a potential dispute involving employees and will better protect an employer who may otherwise be obligated to disclose such records as part of a discovery request. Of course, the implementation of an e-mail policy should not be taken to authorize unrestricted or inappropriate monitoring of employee e-mail. Any monitoring should be in compliance with a written procedure that authorizes such access by designated information system and only upon the prior authorization of senior management. E-mail interception or monitoring should not be used as a fishing expedition or to gain access to personal information or facts about an individual that are unrelated to the performance of an employee's duties.[33]

---

30 For example, Article I, Section 1 of California's state constitution provides an express right to privacy.

31 For example, the torts of unreasonable intrusion into a person's private affairs, public disclosure of private facts and placing someone in a false light.

32 In addition to obtaining employees' acknowledgement of or agreement to the policy, many companies configure their computer systems to display a log-on notice which re-enforces the policy and further negates the expectation of privacy.

33 For instance, to confirm an employee's sexual orientation, health condition or whether a female employee is pregnant.

(b) Retention Policies for E-mail

Finally, an e-mail policy should address retention/deletion issues. For instance, the policy may provide that all e-mail messages will be automatically deleted after a specified period of time unless action is taken by the user to preserve a specific message (for instance, by printing out the message or moving the message to a folder). It should be noted that this runs counter to the way most e-mail systems work.[34]

Policies regarding backups of the e-mail system must also be considered. An important component of a company's e-mail policy should be a requirement that, in addition to regular purges of old mail by the system, copies of deleted e-mail records should not be retained on backup tapes. While a company's e-mail system may be routinely backed up to protect its contents in the event of a crash or malfunction of the system (*i.e.*, for system restoration purposes), historical backup tapes should not be retained. This may require that separate backups be performed for the e-mail system. If a business routinely backs up its entire network, including its e-mail system, and retains backup tapes for a period of years, it potentially exposes itself to horrendous burdens in discovery and may find itself needing to unnecessarily review millions of e-mail messages.[35]

(c) Other Important Components

Another defensive strategy is to replace the use of an e-mail system for certain types of sensitive communications. For instance, work group messaging/collaboration software, that maintains all messages in only one centralized location, can help ensure that additional electronic copies will not be retained when the central copy is deleted (subject to backup policies applicable to copies of the centralized message storage facility).

Other important components include:[36]

- the e-mail system should not be used to communicate personal information or to comment about others;
- messages should be organized by subject so that they can be more easily deleted as a group when no longer required;

---

34 With the exception of UNIX based e-mail systems, that typically purge messages automatically once they have been read, unless a recipient explicitly indicates differently, most corporate e-mail systems will automatically save a copy of a read e-mail message unless it is explicitly deleted by the recipient.

35 *Supra*, at note 17.

36 For further information on drafting an e-mail policy, see Chapter 10 of Gahtan, Kratz and Mann, *Internet Law: A Practical Guide for Legal and Business Professionals* (Toronto: Carswell, 1998).

- ideally, the e-mail system should be configurable to delete all messages after a specified period unless they are archived by the recipient or are designated by the sender as "official" e-mail;
- administrators should run e-mail compression utilities often (*e.g.*, weekly) in order to permanently erase any deleted messages; and
- all employees should be made aware that messages may be subject to production in a lawsuit.

(d) Privilege Issue

In some circumstances, e-mail messages exchanged between employees may be protected by a privilege claim (*e.g.*, where the messages were obtained or prepared in contemplation of litigation).[37] However, where it cannot be shown that the dominant purpose for the creation of the electronic messages was to obtain legal advice or to aid in the conduct of litigation, a claim of privilege may not be available (notwithstanding that the message may have discussed the possibility of settlement but was not communicated to the other party and not written without prejudice).[38]

6.8 EMPLOYEE TRAINING

Because electronic information is typically disseminated more broadly than paper documents, organizations will also need to ensure that employees are properly trained, and that adequate technical precautions are undertaken to maintain confidentiality and privilege applicable to such documents.

An employer should consider educating employees on electronic evidence issues and providing employees with some guidance on the types of messages to be avoided (*i.e.*, sexual comments, sexist or racist jokes, disparaging comments about the company's products, etc.). Employees should be advised when and how to delete e-mail messages from their mailbox. They should also be advised to mark sensitive messages as "confidential" and where appropriate, as "privileged".[39]

If a communication or conclusion is preliminary and would not normally be committed to writing, then its transmission by way of an e-mail message should be avoided. Employees should be advised that e-mail messages are another type of "document" that can be subject to disclosure during litigation. Employees should

---

37 For instance, see *Pedersen v. Westfair Foods Ltd.* (1993), 18 C.P.C. (3d) 291 (B.C. Master).

38 *NRS Block Brothers Realty Ltd. v. Co-operators Development Corp.* (1994), 24 C.P.C. (3d) 132, 119 Sask. R. 279 (Sask. Q.B.).

39 For instance, requests for legal advice, responses to queries from legal counsel concerning a legal dispute, etc.

also be encouraged to use discretion in what they write in an e-mail message and in considering who should be included in the distribution list.

Some companies, such as DuPont, have developed a business writing guide and employee training video for use as a risk mitigation tool.

6.9 ELECTRONIC DISCOVERY RESPONSE PROGRAM

Some companies have developed a comprehensive program for responding to electronic discovery requests. Such a program typically includes:

- designing a document management program that facilitates the identification and preservation of relevant electronic data;
- designating an individual (or group of employees) with special training who can be called upon to assist with electronic evidence production requests, particularly those relating to e-mail; and
- identification of and establishment of a relationship with electronic discovery consultants (and preferably, the conduct of an internal audit and assessment by such consultant).

7

Disclosure Obligations Regarding Electronic Evidence

The obligations discussed in this chapter and the one that follows are based on rules which vary between jurisdictions. Although the discussion that follows is intended to be general in nature, and tends to intermix Canadian and American procedural authorities, there are differences between the two. There may also be differences in respect to the local rules applicable in your specific province or state.

7.1 IMPORTANCE OF OBTAINING DISCLOSURE IN ELECTRONIC FORM

The most desirable goal of litigation counsel should be to obtain direct access to the opposing party's computer system so that an expert can search for and, if necessary, recover or reconstruct relevant electronic files. Access to electronic evidence can reveal information not found and/or not disclosed by the other party. Even if this is not possible, there is still a benefit to obtaining an electronic copy of all relevant documents.

The more data that can be obtained in electronic form, the better. Aside from the possibility of providing valuable and relevant information not revealed in printed copies, they can also facilitate the entry of the information into counsel's litigation support system. In the case of database files, it can allow a lawyer to process or examine the data in different ways without providing an insight about his or her trial strategy to the opposing side. Searching for certain types of trends or relationships may only be possible where access to the relevant data is available in electronic form.[1] In some cases, data in electronic form may be required in order

---

1 See *Ball v. State*, 101 Misc.2d 554, 421 N.Y.S.2d 328 (N.Y.Ct.Cl., 1979), where a court permitted the plaintiff to use the defendant's computerized database of auto accident records in order to analyze traffic accident patterns, and build a case that a road's design

to permit experts to run certain simulations.[2] Also, it allows a lawyer to explore questions that might otherwise have been too expensive or time consuming to answer.

7.2   DISCLOSURE OBLIGATIONS EXTEND TO EVIDENCE IN ELECTRONIC FORM

Today it is black letter law that computerized data is discoverable if relevant.[3]

In Ontario, each party has an obligation to identify and list in an affidavit of documents all documents relevant to the matters at issue in the proceeding that are or have been in the party's possession, power or control. The threshold for relevancy at this stage in the proceeding is low.

In the United States, the general rule respecting discovery is that each party to an action is bound to produce all documents in its possession, and to disclose all facts within its knowledge, that are material to the other party's case. A "broad relevance" test is applicable at the document production phase. The general principle is that a party is entitled to discovery of a document or record if it directly, or indirectly, enables it to advance its own case or to destroy that of its adversary; or, may fairly lead to a train of inquiry that may have either of these consequences.[4]

The scope of what is discoverable is also broad in the United States. Rule 26(b)(1) of the *Federal Rules of Civil Procedure* provides:

> Parties may obtain discovery regarding any matter not privileged, which is relevant to the subject matter involved in the pending action, whether it relates to the claim or defense of the party seeking discovery or to the claim or defense of any other party, including the existence, description, nature, custody, condition, and location of any books, documents, or other tangible things and the identity and location of persons having knowledge of any discoverable matter.

---

was faulty.

2   *In re Air Crash Disaster at Detroit Metropolitan Airport on Aug. 16, 1987*, 130 F.R.D. 634 (E.D.Mich., 1989). The co-defendant was successful in obtaining access to data stored on a nine-track tape because it was able to convince the court that it would be extremely difficult for its expert to form an informed opinion as to certain aspects of the flight without the data.

3   *Anti-Monopoly, Inc. v. Hasbro, Inc.*, 94 Civ. 2120, 1995 WL 649934 (S.D.N.Y., 1995).

4   *Bank of Montreal v. 3D Properties Inc.*, [1993] S.J. No. 278 (Sask. Q.B.), citing various authorities.

In the United States, Rule 34 of the *Federal Rules of Civil Procedure* was amended in 1970 to clarify that the discovery of information in new media, including computer-based media, is both necessary and proper. In early cases that followed the change, US courts held that computer tapes were the proper subject of discovery.[5] Also, as early as 1977, the Manual of Complex Litigation (CCH) [2.715] recognized the production of computerized information in machine-readable form as the primary mode of responding to discovery requests in complex cases, with the production of printouts as a secondary alternative.

Recent cases have confirmed that computer-based data is discoverable if relevant[6] and that courts may also penalize a party for failing to produce electronic evidence.[7]

In *C.M. Security Components Ltd. v. Canada*,[8] in discussing the requirements under the *Federal Rules of Practice*, the court stated:

> Clearly, what is relevant for the purpose of preparing for a trial is any document which might reasonably be supposed to contain information which may directly or indirectly enable the party requiring production to advance his own case or to damage the case of his adversary.

While this chapter reviews some of the developments relating to the discoverability of electronic evidence, it now appears well settled that disclosure obligations do extend to data in electronic form. The challenge now lies in defining the scope of discovery and the allocation of costs associated with it.

(a) Electronic Data as "Documents"

A party involved in litigation must identify and, if not privileged, produce to the other parties copies of all relevant documents.[9] Disclosure must be made of every document relating to a matter in issue in an action that is, or has been, in the

---

5 For instance, see *Adams v. Dan River Mills, Inc.*, 54 F.R.D. 220 (W.D.Va., 1972); *U.S. v. Davey*, 543 F.2d 996 (2nd Cir. (N.Y.), 1976).

6 *Anti-Monopoly, Inc. v. Hasbro, Inc.*, 94 Cir. 2120, 1995 U.S. Dist. Lexis 16355 (S.D.N.Y., 1995). See also, *Seattle Audubon Society v. Lyons*, 871 F. Supp. 1291 (W.D. Wash., 1994), judgment affirmed by *Seattle Audubon Soc. v. Moseley*, 80 F.3d 1401 (9th Cir. (Wash.), 1996) where the court ordered the production of e-mail.

7 See *American Bankers Ins. Co. of Florida v. Caruth*, 786 S.W.2d 427 (Tex.App.-Dallas, 1990).

8 [1994] F.C.J. No. 732 (Fed. T.D.).

9 For instance, Rule 401 of the *Federal Rules of Evidence* in the United States provides that "relevant evidence" means evidence having any tendency to make the existence of any fact that is of consequence to the determination of the action more probable or less probable than it would be without the evidence.

possession, power or control of a party.[10] Although documents are commonly thought of as meaning paper documents, the definition of documents for the purposes of discovery can be very broad and may include photographs, videotape and computer-based[11] evidence. The fact that certain documents or records are in electronic rather than paper form does not mean a party can avoid disclosing them.

In most jurisdictions, the definition of "document" has been specifically broadened to include computer data, however generated or stored. Even before legislative changes, the courts had generally interpreted the definition of document to include computer-generated data.

Proctor & Gamble Co. v. Kimberly-Clark of Can. Ltd.,[12] involved an application by the plaintiff for an order to inspect and make copies of computer tapes listed in the defendant's list of documents. The defendant acknowledged that the computer tapes were "documents" and that the plaintiff was entitled to take a copy of such tapes. However, the defendant argued that it would be adequate for it to provide the plaintiff with a copy of everything contained in the computer tape in human readable form. The plaintiff argued that the human readable form would require "a room the size of the courtroom" in which to store. The court held that, pursuant to Rule 453 of the *Federal Court Rules* (Canada), the plaintiff was entitled to a copy of the computer tapes along with any other information that was necessary to obtain the information required from the tapes. Rule 453, as it then was, provided:

> 453(1). A party who has served a list of documents on any other party . . . shall allow the other party to inspect the documents referred to in the list (other than any which he objects to produce or which are not in his possession, custody or power) and to take copies thereof; and, accordingly, he shall when he serves the list on the other party also serve on him a notice stating a time within 15 days after the service thereof when such of the said documents as he has possession or control of may be inspected at a place specified in the notice . . .[13]

The court had noted that the defendant's list of documents clearly stipulated computer tapes as some of the documents it may use for trial purposes. The court stated that this means anything on the computer tape could have been used. Therefore, disclosure was warranted.

---

10 In Ontario, see Rule 30.02 of the *Rules of Civil Procedure* (the "Rules").

11 The definition of "document" in Rule 30.01(1) of the Rules includes "information recorded or stored by means of any device." In the United States, the definition of a "document" under the *Federal Rules of Civil Procedure* 34(a) expressly includes electronic information. Magnetically or electronically recorded data is also considered a writing or recording under Rule 1001(1) of the *Federal Rules of Evidence* (US).

12 (1989), 25 C.P.R. (3d) 244 (Fed. T.D.).

13 The *Federal Court Rules* have since been revised. The corresponding rule in the *Ontario Rules of Civil Procedure* is Rule 30.04.

Bank of Montreal v. 3D Properties Inc.,[14] involved an application by one of the defendants for production by the plaintiff of various documents. The court had to consider Rule 211 of the court's *Rules of Practice and Procedure*, which read:

> "document" includes information recorded or stored by means of any device and includes an audio recording, video recording, computer disc, film, photograph, chart, graph, map, plan, survey, book of account or machine readable information.

The court interpreted the word "document", as used and defined by Rule 211, as being broad enough to include "information stored on computer hard drive discs, and, as well, on other (hard) computer records, including tape backup, and other information storing devices such as word processing equipment, electronic diaries and/or electronic notebooks." However, the court set the following conditions:

- the plaintiff would be entitled to first edit all information that is clearly protected against disclosure as being privileged and confidential;
- the plaintiff would not be required to alter the format of the data contained in any computer records, discs, and/or tapes, and is only obligated to produce copies of same (as edited) to the applicant in its present existing form; and
- all reasonable costs incurred by the plaintiff, including searching for, locating, editing, and producing the requested documents, would be at the applicant's cost and expense. An estimate would also need to be first provided to the applicant.

Courts in other jurisdictions also generally interpreted "document" to include evidence in electronic form. In *Alliance and Leicester Building Society v. Ghahremani*,[15] a solicitor breached an order by deliberately deleting part of a document stored on the hard disk of his office computer and then attempting to cover his tracks. The court rejected the defendant's arguments that the reference in the order to "documents" should be restricted to a visible writing on paper and not include information stored in the hard disk of a computer.

In *Derby & Co. Ltd. v. Weldon (No 9)*,[16] after holding that a computer database, which formed part of the business records of a company, is a document of which discovery must be given, the court discussed factors that may be considered in the exercise of its discretion:

> . . . expert evidence as to the extent to which the relevant information was available on-line or from back-up systems, archival or history files, the extent

---

14 [1993] S.J. No. 279 (Sask. Q.B.).
15 [1992] R.V.R. 198 (Eng. Ch. Div.).
16 [1991] 2 All E.R. 901 (Eng. Ch. Div.).

to which materials stored in history files could be recovered with or without reprogramming, the extent to which reprogramming and transferring data onto the on-line system might damage the history files of the computer and the extent to which recovery of information and any necessary reprogramming might disrupt the other side's businesses.

(b) Where Available/Disclosed in Paper Form

Litigants should request an inspection[17] and copy[18] of the electronic version of any relevant documents including ones being provided in paper form. As early as 1977, the Manual of Complex Litigation (CCH) [2.715] recognized the production of computerized information in machine-readable form as the primary mode of responding to discovery requests in complex cases, with the production of printouts as a secondary alternative. While not necessarily required, the willingness of the requesting party to pay for the cost of such production may positively influence a court to make such an order.[19]

Courts may be receptive to ordering disclosure in electronic form even when evidence is otherwise available to the requesting party in paper form because of the substantial expense of converting it to computer-readable form for analysis.[20] In *Anti-Monopoly, Inc. v. Hasbro, Inc.*,[21] the defendants objected to production on the grounds that (i) they were producing the information in hard copy form, and (ii) they would have to "create" the information in electronic form. The court stated that the law makes it clear that:

> . . . data in computerized form is discoverable even if paper "hard copies" of the information have been produced, and that the producing party can be required to design a computer program to extract the data from its computer-

---

17 In Ontario, Rule 30.04(7) provides that "A party who serves on another party a request to inspect documents (Form 30C) is entitled to inspect any document that is not privileged and that is referred to in the other party's affidavit of documents as being in the party's possession, control or power". See also *Alberta Rule of the Court*, Rule 189.

18 Rule 30.04(7) of the Rules provides that "Where a document is produced for inspection, the party inspecting the document is entitled to make a copy of it . . ."

19 See *National Union Elec. Corp. v. Matsushita Elec. Indus. Co., Ltd.*, 494 F.Supp. 1257 (E.D.Pa., 1980).

20 *The Manual for Complex Litigation*, 2nd ed. (1986), in section 21.446 states: "Sometimes, a party should be required to provide [this information] in machine-readable form, so that the data may be stored by the discovering parties for later analysis on their own computers without the time, expense, and potential for errors that would result if data from a print-out were re-entered manually." See also *In re Air Crash Disaster at Detroit Metropolitan Airport on Aug. 16, 1987, supra*, at note 2—after producing a printout of a simulation, the party was also required to produce an electronic copy; *National Union Elec. Corp. v. Matsushita Elec. Indus. Co., Ltd., ibid.*

21 *Supra*, at note 3.

ized business records, subject to the Court's discretion as to the allocation of the costs of designing such a computer program.

Applying this principle, the court rejected the defendants' objections. It went on to state:

> Thus, the rule is clear: production of information in "hard copy" documentary form does not preclude a party from receiving the same information in computerized/electronic form.

However, due to certain factual issues regarding the availability of the electronic records, the court ordered the parties to discuss the matter further in light of its ruling. It noted that further rulings could depend on the plaintiff's willingness to pay the defendants' costs in creating the required computer programs that were necessary to extract the requested data.

In some cases, another reason a party may want access to the electronic version is in order to examine information that is not present in the paper version of a document. For instance, in *Reichmann v. Toronto Life Publishing Co.*,[22] the defendant produced a printed copy of a manuscript but the plaintiff insisted on a copy of the electronic version in order to search for information not contained in the printed version. The court concurred and held that the computer disk fell within the wider definition of a document and had to be produced—a printout would not suffice.

However, there have been instances where courts have declined to order production in electronic form after data was already provided in non-electronic form.[23]

---

22 66 O.R. (2d) 65, [1988] O.J. No. 1727, (sub nom. *Reichmann v. Toronto Life Publishing Co. (No. 2))* 30 C.P.C. (2d) 280 (Ont. H.C.). The defendant was ordered to produce a copy of her manuscript (including the current and earlier versions) and certain documents from which she was allowed to first delete references to confidential sources of information. The defendant provided a printout of the manuscript but resisted production of the disk itself. The plaintiff claimed that the deletions made went beyond references to confidential sources and moved to require production of the computer disk. The court held that the computer disk fell within the common law meaning of "document" and had to be produced. See also *Joseph Pruner Ltd. v. Ford Motor Co. of Canada*, [1992] O.J. No. 88 (Ont. Gen. Div.)—a decision that followed *Reichmann* and involved the court ordering production of computer data stored on magnetic tape.

23 *Williams v. Owens-Illinois, Inc.*, 665 F.2d 918 (9th Cir. (Cal.), 1982), *certiorari* denied by *Owens Illinois, Inc. v. Williams*, 459 U.S. 971 (U.S. Cal., 1982). However, this ruling was criticized in Horning, "Electronically Storing Evidence: Answers to Some Recurring Questions Concerning Pretrial Discovery and Trial Use" *Wash. & Lee L. Rev.* 41:1335 (1984). See also *Polansky Electronics Ltd. v. AGT Ltd.* (1997), 205 A.R. 43, 73 C.P.R. (3d) 257 (Alta. Q.B.), where the court held that electronic evidence was not producible as part of documentary discovery where the party had reviewed computer files and had been provided with copies of documents requested from those files.

(c) Where Not Available/Disclosed in Paper Form

US courts have required production of information contained in a computer database even if such data is not available in hard copy form.[24] They have also held "deleted" files contained on a hard disk to be discoverable and have granted a plaintiff's consultant access to a defendant's hard disk to retrieve such files.[25]

(d) Disclosure in Useable Form

Disclosure of electronic data must also be made in a "reasonably usable form" such that the requesting party is able to access the data.[26] For instance, the Advisory Committee notes to the 1970 Amendment to the *Federal Rules of Civil Procedure* (US provide):

> . . . Rule 34 applies to electronic data compilations from which information can be obtained only with the use of detection devices, and [. . .] when data can as a practical matter be made usable by the discovering party only through respondent's devices, respondent may be required to use his devices to translate the data into usable form . . . Similarly, if the discovering party needs to check the electronic source itself, the court may protect respondent with respect to preservation of his records, confidentiality of nondiscoverable matters, and costs.

In Canada, obligations have been imposed on litigants to explain their filing system and to reasonably label documents in a manner that will facilitate their use by the other party.[27] Applied to computerized data, this may mean that a party is obligated to disclose its filing and organization system.

---

24 *Crown Life Ins. Co. v. Craig*, 995 F.2d 1376, 26 Fed.R.Serv. 3d 113 (7th Cir. (Ill.), 1993).

25 *Easley, McCaleb & Assoc. v. Brian A. Perry*, No. E-26663 (Ga.Supr.Ct., 1994).

26 *Greyhound Computer Corp., Inc. v. IBM*, 3 Computer L. Serv. Rep. 138 (D.Minn., 1971)—the defendant was required by the court to supply personnel and materials to assist the plaintiff in accessing computer tapes. See also *Pearl Brewing Co. v. Jos. Schlitz Brewing Co.*, 415 F.Supp. 1122 (S.D. Tex., 1976)—the court ordered production of system documentation.

27 *Canadian Engineering & Surveys (Yukon) Ltd. v. Banque Nationale de Paris (Canada)* (1996), 8 C.P.C. (4th) 190 (Alta. C.A.), affirming (1995), 43 C.P.C. (3d) 277 (Alta. Q.B.); *Saskatachewan Trust Co. (Liquidator of) v. Coopers & Lybrand* (1997), 8 C.P.C. (4th) 238 (Sask. Q.B.); *Solid Waste Reclamation Inc. v. Philip Enterprises Inc.* (1991), 2 O.R. (3d) 481 (Ont. Gen. Div.).

(e) Third Party Software Issues

An interesting issue arises where a requesting party may be entitled to certain electronic evidence that is stored in a proprietary format used by a third party software program, and where such program is not reasonably capable of outputting such information in any industry standard format.[28] Numerous issues may arise:

- The licensee of the third party software program may be contractually bound by the applicable licence agreement not to permit use of the program by a person other than an employee. Depending on the confidentiality provision contained in such licence agreement, the licensee may even be prohibited from operating the program in the presence of a non-employee.
- The licensee may be able to provide an electronic copy of the data but restricted from providing any information it may have in respect of the data format that might assist the requesting party in accessing the electronic data or importing it into another software program for analysis.
- In some cases, the licence agreement may stipulate that the data itself contains confidential information or trade secrets of the licensor that would be disclosed by a disclosure of the data.

The disclosing party may, therefore, be precluded by contract and copyright law from providing the requesting party with meaningful disclosure. In these circumstances, the requesting party may need to contact and negotiate with the third party licensor in order to facilitate access to the desired information.

7.3 SCOPE AND COST OF ELECTRONIC DISCOVERY

In re Brand Name Prescription Drugs Antitrust Litigation,[29] involved a motion to compel the defendant, CIBA-Geigy Corporation to produce responsive, computer-stored electronic mail at its own expense. The court granted the motion, subject to certain limitations. In that case, the defendant did not dispute that it had responsive e-mail that was discoverable, but rather argued that the request was "untimely, overly-broad and overly-burdensome" or in the alternative, that the plaintiff should be required to narrow the scope of their request and bear the costs of production.

---

28 See *Middlekamp v. Fraser Valley Real Estate Board* (1990), 29 C.P.R. (3d) 385 (B.C. Master), affirmed (1990), 32 C.P.R. (3d) 206 (B.C. S.C), for an example where a computer program required to prepare requested reports was in the possession and control of a third party. On appeal, the B.C. Supreme Court did not agree with the master's reasoning on the issue, but did agree with his refusal to order production. The court found that the reports being requested were not in existence and that even if the defendant had possession or control of the appropriate software, or could obtain it by simply asking a third party, it could not agree that it was the defendant's duty to create new documents for the benefit of the plaintiff.

29 1995 U.S. Dist. LEXIS 8281 (N.D.Ill., 1995).

The defendant estimated that it had at least 30 million pages of e-mail data stored on its backup tapes and would need to incur $50,000 to $70,000 in compiling, formatting, searching and retrieving responsive e-mail. It argued that the plaintiff should be required to reimburse the defendant for its costs.

The court agreed that the *Manual for Complex Litigation* lends some support to the defendant's position that the plaintiff should be forced to incur the e-mail retrieval and production costs. [30] However, the court found that relevant case law:

> . . . instructs that the mere fact that the production of computerized data will result in a substantial expense is not sufficient justification for imposing the costs of production on the requesting party. Rather, in addition to considering whether the amount of money involved in producing the discovery is inordinate and excessive, the court may consider factors such as whether the relative expense and burden in obtaining the data would be greater to the requesting party as compared to the responding party, and whether the responding party will benefit to some degree in producing the data in question.[31]

The court went on to state that central to any determination of whether a cost should be shifted to a producing party is the issue of whether the expense or burden is "undue":

> On the one hand, it seems unfair to force a party to bear the lofty expense attendant to creating a special computer program for extracting data responsive to a discovery request. On the other hand, if a party chooses an electronic storage method, the necessity for a retrieval program or method is an ordinary and foreseeable risk.

The court cited *Daewoo Electronics Co. v. U.S.*,[32] where the United States Court of International Trade remarked:

> It would be a dangerous development in the law if new techniques for easing the use of information became a hindrance to discovery or disclosure in litigation. The use of excessive technical distinctions is inconsistent with the guiding principle that information which is stored, used, or transmitted in new

---

30 *The Manual for Complex Litigation*, 2nd ed., §21.446 (1993) provides: "Parties sometimes request production in a form that can be created only at substantial expense for additional programming; if so, payment of such costs by the requesting party should be made a condition of production. Indeed, parties obtaining information from another's computerized data typically are required to bear any special expense incident to this form of production."

31 Citing *Bills v. Kennecott Corp.*, 108 F.R.D. 459 (D.Utah, 1985).

32 10 C.I.T. 754, 650 F.Supp. 1003 (CIT, 1986) at 1006.

forms should be available through discovery with the same openness as traditional forms. . . . The normal and reasonable translation of electronic data into a form usable by the discovering party should be the ordinary and foreseeable burden of a respondent in the absence of a showing of extraordinary hardship.

The court held that the defendant's estimated retrieval expenses of $50,000 to $70,000 was not a burden the plaintiff should bear, particularly where "the costliness of the discovery procedure involved is . . . a product of the defendant's record-keeping scheme over which the [plaintiffs have] no control." It should be noted that in this particular case:

- the defendant admitted that part of the burden attendant to searching its storage files resulted from the limitations of the software it was using; and
- four other defendants had produced e-mail without insisting that the plaintiff first agree to pay retrieval costs.

However, the court did order that the plaintiff pay for e-mail selected for copying (at a rate consistent with an agreement previously made between counsel). The court also ordered the plaintiff to narrow their request. For the purpose of containing costs, the court required "the parties to consult with each other and agree on meaningful limitations on the scope of any e-mail search."

In the United States, limitations on the scope of discovery may be found in Rule 26(b)(2) of the *Federal Rules of Civil Procedure* that provides:

> . . . The frequency or extent of use of the discovery methods otherwise permitted under these rules and by any local rule shall be limited by the court if it determines that . . . (iii) the burden or expense of the proposed discovery outweighs its likely benefit, taking into account the needs of the case, the amount in controversy, the parties resources, the importance of the issues at stake in the litigation, and the importance of the proposed discovery in resolving the issues.

Similar reasonable limitations on discovery, involving a balancing in allocating the burden and determining the scope of discovery, are conducted by Canadian courts. For instance, in *Morgan Guaranty Trust Co. of New York v. Outerbridge*,[33] a plaintiff bank that had sued to recover money allegedly credited to defendant's account by mistake. The plaintiff was only obliged to produce any document or entry that was relevant to the matter of handling the accounts involved. The Ontario Supreme Court held that a request by the defendant for more general documents

---

33 (1987), 23 C.P.C. (2d) 127 (Ont. Master), affirmed (1988), 23 C.P.C. (2d) 127n (Ont. H.C.).

(relating to systems operation and procedures), only relevant to a theory unsupported by actual evidence and not pleaded, was too wide and was not justified (there was no evidence that any entry had been deleted).

7.4 SANCTIONS FOR FAILING TO PRODUCE

A court may exercise its discretion in a way so as to penalize a party for failing to produce relevant evidence.[34] For instance, *Lubrizol Corp. v. Imperial Oil Ltd.*[35] involved an application by the defendant for an order granting it leave to introduce additional evidence. In that case, the court declined to exercise its discretion to permit the applicant to submit further evidence partly because much of the further evidence, which included technical information such as "batch data and electronic mail", had been requested by counsel for the plaintiffs on discovery, but had not been produced.

In a case involving an egregious breach of disclosure obligations, a court may grant default judgment.[36] For instance, *Crown Life Ins. Co. v. Craig*[37] involved a counter-claim in which the defendant's expert required certain data for its calculations, but where the plaintiff claimed that only summary documents were available. The plaintiff provided an affidavit stating that there were no underlying documents to support those summaries and all documents responsive to the request had been produced. Without this data, the defendant was not able to contest the plaintiff's calculations of commissions due.

During trial, the plaintiff's witness testified on cross-examination about a database containing raw data of the type originally sought by the defendant. The court found that this database had been used by the plaintiff to prepare its own witness and had planned to use the raw data to rebut the defendant's counter-claim. After finding that the plaintiff had violated discovery orders, the court entered a default judgment in favour of the defendant on the counter-claim.

---

34 *Alberta Rules of Court* 195 provides: (1) Any party omitting to mention any document in his affidavit of documents or any party not producing any document in compliance with a demand may not afterwards use the document in evidence, unless he satisfies the court that he had some sufficient cause for the omission of the document; (2) If any party who has made discovery of documents as provided by these Rules, discovers or comes into possession of any document not previously disclosed and which is relevant to the matters in question in the action or proceeding he shall forthwith give notice thereof to the opposite party, and forthwith upon request shall supply the opposite party with a copy thereof, but in any case the court may permit the document to be given in evidence upon such terms as to costs or otherwise as may be just. In Ontario, see Rule 30.08 of the *Rules of Civil Procedure.*

35 [1994] F.C.J. No. 600 (Fed. T.D.).

36 For another example, see *American Bankers Ins. Co. of Florida v. Caruth*, 786 S.W.2d 427 (Tex.App.—Dallas, 1990).

37 *Supra*, at note 24.

The plaintiff appealed, challenging that the sanction was too harsh and an abuse of discretion. It tried to argue that the request was not specific enough to include the raw data and that its failure to produce was, therefore, not wilful or in bad faith, and therefore did not justify default judgment against it. The Court of Appeal did not agree. It found that a request for "summaries or calculations of renewal commissions" and "documents relating to the calculation of commissions" were sufficient to include the raw data supporting the summaries provided by the plaintiff.

The plaintiff also tried to argue that the data were not "documents" because they were never in any hard copy form, and that the defendant had requested "written documents". However, this argument was also not accepted as the Advisory Committee notes to the 1970 amendment of Rule 34 of the *Federal Rule of Civil Procedure* made it clear that computer data is included in Rule 34's description of documents. In affirming the default judgment sanction, the Court of Appeal also noted that:

> Even if we accept, for the purposes of this discussion, that at the time [the defendant] requested the data [the plaintiff] could not access the data, [the plaintiff] is not relieved from its responsibility to make the data available. Rule 34 contemplates that when data is in an inaccessible form, the party responding to the request for documents must make the data available.

7.5 INSPECTION AND SEIZURE

In applicable cases, litigants should attempt to obtain an inspection of the other party's computer system in order to search for evidence that was hidden, deleted, or not produced, and for evidence of tampering with the evidence that was produced. In Ontario, a court may make an order for the inspection of real or personal property (as part of the normal discovery process) where it appears to be necessary for the proper determination of an issue in a proceeding.[38] For instance, the court may:

- authorize entry on or into and the taking of temporary possession of any property in the possession of a party or a person not a party;
- permit the measuring, surveying or photographing of the property in question, or any particular object or operation on the property; and
- permit the taking of samples, the making of observations or the conducting of tests or experiments.

---

38 In Ontario, see Rule 32.01(1) of the *Rules of Civil Procedure*. A similar rule, Rule 34 of the *Federal Rules of Civil Procedure* in the United States, provides that parties to a lawsuit are permitted to request an inspection of the premises of the opposing party. See also *Alberta Rules of Court* 468.

A court may be more inclined to permit a physical inspection of the opposing party's computer system if it can be shown that the opposing party lacks adequate skills to conduct a reasonable search. A court may also be more inclined to permit discovery of the other party's computerized files where the other party fails to take appropriate actions to preserve electronic evidence in their possession (for instance, by failing to make proper image backups).[39] A subsequent discovery of additional relevant documents not disclosed in the affidavit of documents may furnish proof of such a lack of sufficient skills.

US courts have also issued *ex parte* orders (known as *Anton Piller* orders in Canada) permitting the seizure of computer equipment and software from a defendant's premises;[40] particularly where required to prevent the defendant from destroying evidence before discovery can occur,[41] or to prevent a further use of misappropriated information and trade secrets,[42] or infringement of intellectual property rights.

Alliance and Leicester Building Society v. Ghahremani[43] concerned a motion to commit to prison for contempt of court a solicitor who was in breach of an order that had been served upon him. With the assistance of its computer expert, the plaintiff was able to prove beyond a reasonable doubt that the defendant had altered or destroyed a crucial document (in breach of the order of the court to preserve relevant documents).[44] The court was also able to find that the defendant had compounded his misconduct by subsequently forging a document in an attempt to hide his tampering.

---

39 See *Gates Rubber Co. v. Bando Chemical Industries, Ltd.*, 167 F.R.D. 90 (D. Colo., 1996). In this case, an employee of the defendant admitted that he had "cleaned up" his word processing files shortly after learning of the allegations against the defendant, but claimed that he did not erase any materials that were relevant to the litigation. The court permitted the plaintiff to copy the defendant's hard drive in order to try and recover as much of the deleted material as possible (and in fact that plaintiff was able to recover a number of these deleted files). However, see *Eugene J. Strasser, M.D., P.A. v. Bose Yalamanchi, M.D., P.A.*, 669 So.2d 1142 (Fla.App. 4 Dist., 1996), where the District Court of Appeal quashed a trial court's discovery order on the basis that (1) the proposed order permitting unrestricted access to the defendant's entire computer system was overly broad and would pose a threat to patients' confidential records and the records of the defendant's entire business, and (2) there was little evidence that the evidence in question, that had been purged, could be retrieved. In order to permit such a search, the plaintiff would need to demonstrate a likelihood of retrieving the purged information and that there was no less intrusive method to retrieve it.

40 See *Religious Technology Centre v. F.A.C.T. NET Inc.*, 901 F.Supp 1519 (D.Colo., 1995).

41 See *Quotron Systems, Inc. v. Automatic Data Processing, Inc.*, 141 F.R.D. 37 (S.D.N.Y., 1992).

42 See *First Technology Safety Systems, Inc. v. Depinet*, 11 F.3d 641 (6th Cir. (Ohio), 1993).

43 [1992] R.V.R. 198 (Eng. Ch. Div.).

44 The plaintiff was able to show that the file in question was last "saved" at the time that the defendant had been using the computer.

Some courts have acknowledged that the discovery of electronic evidence on an opponent's computer system may be within the scope of the rules of discovery and appropriate in some cases, but may not be willing to order the discovery of such data without a showing of a "particularized likelihood of discovering appropriate information",[45] or that such discovery would lead to evidence that had not already been produced.[46] In some cases, courts may order production of electronic evidence, including e-mail, but may place limitations on the scope of the search and may permit the disclosing party to recover its costs of any copies that are requested.[47] A court may also be reluctant to order electronic discovery where the likelihood of recovering deleted data is low and permitting broad access to an opponent's computer system could cause irreparable harm (*e.g.*, where such system is used to store confidential patient information).[48]

7.6 CONFIDENTIALITY ISSUES

. . . [T]he necessity for confidentiality itself is not a reason recognized in law for refusing to produce a document. The Court can make orders restricting the use of the document . . .[49]

In some cases, issues of confidentiality or proprietary information will arise in respect of the disclosure of certain types of electronic evidence (for instance, computer source code). However, generally courts are reluctant to restrict disclosure of information to the parties.[50]

In cases where confidentiality is an issue, courts may make a protective order. In the United States, Rule 26(c) of the *Rules of Civil Procedure* provides:

---

45 See *Fennell v. First Step Designs Ltd.*, 83 F.3d 526 (1st Cir. (Me.), 1996).

46 See *Lawyers Title Ins. Corp. v. U.S. Fidelity & Guar. Co.*, 122 F.R.D. 567 (N.D. Cal., 1988).

47 See *In re Brand Name Prescription Drug Antitrust Litigation*, 94-C-897, M.D.L. 997 (N.D. Ill. 1995). There are also Canadian cases regarding payment for the reasonable costs of discovery.

48 See *Eugene J. Strasser, M.D., P.A. v. Bose Yalamachi, M.D., P.A., supra*, at note 39. However, concerns regarding confidentiality may be overcome by an appropriate agreement to limit disclosure and/or use of a third party expert to conduct the initial review.

49 *Morgan Guaranty Trust Co. of New York v. Outerbridge, supra*, at note 33.

50 See *Deprenyl Research Ltd. v. Canguard Health Technologies Inc.* (1992), 41 C.P.R. (3d) 228 (Fed. T.D.); *Devron-Hercules Inc. v. Gill* (1988), 21 C.P.R. (3d) 455 (B.C. C.A.), where the court was concerned that it would not likely be able to contain the confidentiality of the information and that the probative value was not sufficient to outweigh the potential harm.

> Upon motion by a party or by the person from whom discovery is sought . . .
> and for good cause shown, the court in which the action is pending or
> alternatively, on matters relating to a deposition, the court in the district where
> the deposition is to be taken place may make any order which justice requires
> to protect a party or person from annoyance, embarrassment, oppression, or
> undue burden or expense, including one or more of the following: (1) that the
> disclosure or discovery not be had; (2) that the disclosure or discovery may be
> had only on specified terms and conditions, including a designation of the time
> or place; (3) that the discovery may be had only by a method of discovery other
> than that selected by the party seeking discovery; (4) that certain matters not
> be inquired into, or that the scope of the disclosure or discovery be limited to
> certain matters; . . . (7) that a trade secret or other confidential research,
> development, or commercial information not be revealed or be revealed only
> in a designated way . . .

The Advisory Committee note to the *Federal Rules of Civil Procedure* 34, as
amended in 1970, provides, in part:

> . . . if the discovering party needs to check the electronic source itself, the court
> may protect respondent with respect to preservation of his records, confiden-
> tiality of nondiscoverable matters, and costs.

Canadian courts dealt with this issue in *Altec Design Group Ltd. v. Motion Works
Inc.*[51] This case involved competing claims for copyright with each party claiming
ownership of source code in respect of computer programs. The issue was how the
details of each party's code could be disclosed for the purposes of determining any
similarities and differences while preserving the interest in retaining exclusive
knowledge of those details. The court held that each party was to retain an expert
to inspect the code of the adverse party, and that the expert and solicitor were to
give a written undertaking on the confidentiality aspect of their review.

The court reviewed numerous authorities, that are summarized into the following
principles:[52]

---

51 [1992] B.C.J. No. 2451 (B.C. Master).
52 *Forestral Automation Ltd. v. R.M.S. Industrial Controls Inc.* (1977), 4 B.C.L.R. 219,
    80 D.L.R. (3d) 41, 35 C.P.R. (2d) 114 (B.C. S.C.); *Devron-Hercules Inc. v. Gill, supra*,
    at note 50; *GEAC Can. Ltd. v. Prologic Computer Corp.* (1989), 24 C.P.R. (3d) 566
    (B.C. S.C.); *Webster v. Mastercraft Development Corp.* (1991), 55 B.C.L.R. (2d) 121
    (B.C. C.A. [In Chambers]); *Deprenyl Research Ltd. v. Canguard Health Technologies
    Inc., supra*, at note 50; *G.W.L. Properties Ltd. v. W.R. Grace & Co. of Canada* (1992),
    70 B.C.L.R. (2d) 180 (B.C. S.C.).

- The necessity for complete disclosure in litigation cases supersedes the fact that a party may lose a competitive advantage when disclosure is made.[53]
- In maintaining a balance between disclosure and confidentiality, the governing principal is to lean in favour of openness and disclosure.[54]
- The party viewing the confidential materials shall give an undertaking to the court and the opposite party, the terms of which may vary from case to case.[55]
- The party whose documents are being disclosed to be examined by an expert is entitled to have a representative present during the examination.[56]
- An order preventing counsel from showing relevant documents to his client should only be granted in exceptional circumstances.[57]
- The onus is on the party requesting the restriction to establish a legal reason for the restriction.[58]
- In matters that do not require technical expertise, the parties may be required to produce the documents to a third party for the examination and report to the court.[59]
- In instances where the probative value of the documents is not sufficiently great to outweigh the real and considerable adverse effect of disclosing the trade secret, disclosure ought not to be ordered.[60]

The court held that while full disclosure is the general rule and is to be encouraged, it was of the view that the proper procedure to be followed in this case was for each party's expert to review that party's own product with their own technicians. Once having accomplished that, to review the other's source code and object codes and then to make their report, with a copy to be delivered to the adverse party. Such examination was ordered to be made in the absence of technicians but with a representative from the adverse party present (if that party so chooses). The court stated that in the event that the expert cannot complete his or her report without consultation with its own technicians and disclosing the other's source or object codes to the party's technicians, then another application may be made to vary the order, provided that the expert has a legitimate need to consult those technicians and can convince the presiding master or judge that such disclosure is necessary.[61]

---

53 *Forestral Automation Ltd. v. R.M.S. Industrial Controls Inc., ibid.*

54 *Deveron-Hercules Inc. v. Gill, supra*, at note 50.

55 *GEAC Can. Ltd. v. Prologic Computer Corp., supra*, at note 52.

56 *Ibid.*

57 *Deprenyl Research Ltd. v. Canguard Health Technologies Inc. supra*, at note 50.

58 *Ibid.*

59 *Webster v. Mastercraft Development Corporation* (1991), 55 B.C.L.R. (2d) 121 (B.C. C.A. [In Chambers]).

60 *G.W.L. Properties Ltd. v. W.R. Grace & Co. of Canada* (1992), 70 B.C.L.R. (2d) 180 (B.C. S.C.).

61 In this case, the court recognized the importance of maintaining the confidentiality of source code. It stated that "Both counsel described the source and objects codes as a type of 'road map' into the software program", and "Once a technician views the source and object codes, he or she will have a clear understanding of how [the] program was developed and may utilize that knowledge in the development of further software products."

In *Forestral Automation Ltd. v. R.M.S. Industrial Controls Inc.*,[62] the court acknowledged the two rational but opposing arguments that arise in these types of cases:

> For the plaintiff to prove its case it wants to see the alleged secret documents.
> They might advance its position or they might not. If the plaintiff is denied
> access it may lose the action. On the other hand, if it sees them and they are
> in fact what the defendants claim to be then the plaintiff will have gained a
> valuable commercial secret which it would possibly use in its competition with
> the defendants.

The court also reviewed the types of orders that may be made:

1. The legal advisers and experts of the applicants (which may be limited in
    number and subject to the names first being given to the respondent) may
    inspect the documents and make minutes of their contents and be entitled
    to be supplied with copies, subject to such persons undertaking not to
    disclose the result of the inspection to anyone else;
2. The parties agree on a single expert to be given full and unfettered access
    to the material. Evidence of any reports, if called at trial, to be heard on
    camera.
3. The material to be revealed to the party's counsel, technical experts and
    its chief executive officer, each to give an undertaking in writing to the
    respondent and to the court not to divulge the information to others and
    not to use the information or permit it to be used for any purpose other
    than in connection with the action.

In *Forestral Automation Ltd. v. R.M.S. Industrial Controls Inc., supra*, the defendant was ordered to permit inspection by the president of the plaintiff, one legal
advisor of the plaintiff and one other expert to be appointed by the plaintiff. Each
were required to give an undertaking in writing to the court and to the defendant
prior to the inspection that they would not disclose the results of the inspection to
anyone else save through evidence at trial and would not use the information gained
by the inspection for any purpose other than a purpose connected with the action.
Bouck J. stated:[63]

> Notwithstanding the force of the argument that the defendants might lose a
> competitive advantage if the reports and drawings are shown to the plaintiff
> or its experts, I am of the view this contention is second to the necessity for
> complete and open disclosure when it comes to litigation. Otherwise a legiti-
> mate claim could be completely frustrated.

---

62 *Supra*, at note 52.
63 *Ibid.*, (1977), 4 B.C.L.R. 219 at 231, 35 C.P.R. 114 at 124.

In *Devron-Hercules Inc. v. Gill*,[64] disclosure had been made to the plaintiff's solicitor and its expert. On appeal, the plaintiff sought to remove the prohibition in the protective order against disclosure by its lawyers to its officers, claiming that such condition precluded discussions between the plaintiff and its legal advisers on those matters. The court accepted submissions that it was necessary for the expert to discuss with the plaintiff the differences between the inventions described in the plaintiff's patents and that described in the defendant's application. The defendant responded that, however genuine may be the present intention of the plaintiff to use the information only for the purpose of the action, it is impossible for those persons to put out of their minds what they had learned.

The court held that the restrictions create a real risk that the plaintiff could not properly prosecute its action, and that given the nature of the issue, to continue to prohibit the plaintiff's principals from having access to the materials is not justified. An important factual basis for the decision may have been that the court found that only the plaintiff's principals had the background to assess certain technical questions that would be raised by the comparison of the plaintiff's and defendant's designs, and that if their assistance is not available to their expert, there would be the prospect of real and substantial prejudice to the preparation of their case.

The court also stated that "the governing principle in these matters is to lean in favour of openness and disclosure" (p. 459) and that "in striking a balance between openness and disclosure on the one side and the maintenance of confidentiality on the other, our rules and our decisions have given substantially greater weight to the need for disclosure than have the rules and decisions in England." (p. 460)

In *GEAC Can. Ltd. v. Prologic Computer Corp.*,[65] the plaintiffs applied for an order permitting their expert to view the source code of the defendant's system for the purpose of determining whether it was derived from the plaintiffs' rival product and from confidential information gained by the personal defendants during their employment with the plaintiffs. The court ordered the source code be disclosed on the following terms:

- the defendants will be entitled to have an expert or other representative present at all times to observe the viewing of the source code;
- the defendants will be entitled duplicates of any copies made by the plaintiffs' expert;
- the plaintiffs' expert will remain under confidentiality restrictions;
- prior to the plaintiffs' expert discussing what he sees with employees of the plaintiffs (for the purpose of determining whether or not parts of the defen-

---

64 *Supra*, at note 50.
65 *Supra*, at note 52.

dant's source code may be derived from the plaintiffs' confidential product), defendants to be first given notice of what items of source code are to be discussed and the identity of the specific plaintiff's employees. Such employees to first enter into the same undertaking relating to confidentiality, to be in writing and delivered to the solicitors for the defendants. If the defendants have any reason to object to any such person, they may apply to the court. Any such persons may only see the source code in the presence of the plaintiffs' expert; and

- any copies taken of the defendants' source code to be carefully protected and remain in the custody of the plaintiffs' expert at all times. Any copies to be disposed of only by further order of the court at the conclusion of the proceedings. No further copies to be made by others.

A party wishing to resist providing an undertaking of confidentiality may argue that there is sufficient protection to a respondent under the general principles of law, that matters disclosed on discovery may not be made use of other than for the purpose of the litigation in question.[66]

In Ontario, Rule 30.1.01 of the *Rule of Civil Procedure* provides that parties may not use evidence or information obtained through the discovery process for any purposes other than those of the proceeding in which the evidence was obtained. Violation of this deemed undertaking has been treated as a contempt of court. The existence of this implied undertaking has made the making of specific confidentiality orders unnecessary in Ontario. In Alberta, this issue has been addressed extensively in the caselaw, and it is settled law that such an implied undertaking exists.[67]

---

66 *Warner-Lambert Co. v. Glaxo Laboratories*, [1975] R.P.C. 354 (Eng. C.A.) at 362. However, in most cases an undertaking should be given by the applicant so that the respondent's trade secret is protected as far as possible from future infringement, should the applicant fail in its action at trial. (see p. 361 at line 38).

67 For excellent discussions see: *Wirth Ltd. v. Acadia Pipe & Supply Corp.* (1991), 79 Alta. L.R. (2d) 345, 50 C.P.C. (2d) 273 (Alta. Q.B.) and *Ed Miller Sales & Rentals Ltd. v. Caterpillar Tractor Co.* (1986), 43 Alta. L.R. 299 (2d) (Alta. Q.B.). In the *Ed Miller* case, Wachowich J. held that there are three categories of cases with respect to the issue of implied warranty: (i) those cases for which the implied undertaking is sufficient, being the majority of cases; (ii) those cases that merit the requirement that the receiving party be directed to give formal undertakings; and (iii) a small core of cases in which the circumstances warrant further precautionary measures. These cases also reject the British Columbia position that no such implied undertaking arises (see *Kyuquot Logging Ltd. v. B.C. Forest Products Ltd.*, [1986] 5 W.W.R. 481, 30 D.L.R. (4th) 65 (B.C. C.A.).

7.7 PRODUCTION OF SPECIFIC TYPES OF EVIDENCE

(a) E-mail

E-mail has been a popular category of electronic evidence that has been requested and used in numerous cases. There appears to be little doubt that e-mail evidence is discoverable. For instance, in *In re Brand Name Prescription Drugs Antitrust Litigation*,[68] the court held that e-mail is discoverable pursuant to Rules 26(b) and 34 of the *Federal Rules of Civil Procedure*, that provide that computer-stored information is discoverable under the same rules that pertain to tangible, written materials.

However, the discovery of e-mail evidence may be subject to certain reasonable limits. For instance, in *Bass Public Ltd. Co. v. Promus Companies Inc.*,[69] an order compelling production of documents included a search of the defendant's e-mail system for all e-mail related to 10 individuals to be selected by the plaintiff.

(b) Source Code

GEAC Can. Ltd. v. Prologic Computer Corp.,[70] involved a civil action arising out of an allegation of breach of contract of employment and fiduciary duty due to the development of a computer program by the defendants based on computer designs originally developed by plaintiffs. The plaintiffs applied for an order requiring the defendants to provide, among other things, all magnetic media containing the source code. While the court accepted that magnetic media containing source codes constituted documents, it had to deal with the defendants' position that they might lose a competitive advantage if the reports and drawings relating to the program were shown to the plaintiffs or their experts. The court held that:

> [T]he balance between those competing interests, that is, the interest of the plaintiffs in obtaining information which is relevant to the litigation and the defendants' legitimate interest in not losing its competitive advantage is to be weighed in favor of the plaintiffs.

While the court ordered that all of the copying and information obtained as the result of any inspection, should be treated as confidential and used only for the purposes of that particular litigation, after hearing counsel's submission on the vital nature of the source code materials to the defendants, the court decided to restrict

---

68 *Supra*, at note 29.

69 1994 WL 702052 (S.D.N.Y., 1994).

70 *Supra*, at note 52.

inspection to all documents except the source code and to defer ruling on the inspection of the source code material at that time.[71]

(c) Litigation Support Systems

In some cases, particularly those involving complex litigation, one party may have inputted or organized the relevant documents and information into a litigation support database. Once the discovery process commences, the other party may seek access to this database. Such databases will typically be protected from disclosure under rules of privilege. However, in some cases courts may need to decide whether limited access should be provided.

In *R.J. Reynolds Tobacco Co. v. Minnesota*,[72] the US Supreme Court denied without comment a *certiorari* petition by the defendant tobacco companies, who had requested that the high court overturn Minnesota state court decisions that required the tobacco companies to provide the plaintiff with a copy of their computerized database of litigation-related records.[73]

However, generally courts will be reluctant to order discovery of electronic copies of evidence where such evidence is stored in a computerized litigation support system.[74] Courts may even be reluctant to require disclosure of information about the setup of an opponent's litigation support system.[75] Concern is greatest where such systems incorporate summary or index information, and may reflect the "mental impressions, theories and thought processes"[76] of a party's counsel.[77] However, even with systems that do not incorporate summary or index information, disclosure may still provide the other party with valuable information concerning trial strategy by indicating which documents were thought important enough to

---

71 See also *Altec Design Group Ltd. v. Motion Works Inc.*, *supra*, at note 51, which involved competing claims for copyright with each party claiming ownership of source code in respect of computer programs.

72 116 S.Ct. 1852 (Mem) (U.S.Minn., 1996).

73 The trial decision was *State, By Humphrey v. Philip Morris, Inc.*, 1998 WL 257214 (Minn.Dist.Ct., 1998).

74 Evidence, including electronic evidence, organized by an lawyer may constitute work product and not be discoverable on the grounds of privilege—*Santiago v. Miles*, 121 F.R.D. 636 (W.D.N.Y., 1988). See also Krigbaum, "Computerized Litigation Support Systems and the Attorney Work Product Doctrine: The Need for Court Support Against Discovery", 17 *Val. U.L. Rev.* 281 (1983).

75 *Hoffman v. United Telecommunications, Inc.*, 117 F.R.D. 436 (D.Kan., 1987).

76 The *Federal Rules of Civil Procedure* 26(b)(3) provides that "the court shall protect against the disclosure of the mental impressions, conclusions, opinions, or legal theories of an attorney or other representative of a party concerning the litigation."

77 *In re IBM Peripheral EDP Devices Antitrust Litigation*, 5 Computer L. Serv. Rep. 878 (N.D.Cal., 1975).

track. Any protection may, however, be lost if the system is intended to be used by testifying experts.[78]

R. v. Stewart,[79] involved a murder trial in which the accused, who had been provided with thousands of pages of documentary material (including officers' notes and witnesses' statements), requested a copy in electronic form that the Crown had created. The disclosure included approximately 52,000 pages of documents that had taken about one year to input into electronic form. The accused argued that the Crown's possession of such information in an electronic form constituted a "huge technical advantage" over the defence and impinged on a fair trial.

The court concluded that certain memoranda of police officers constituted protected work product of the Crown and that the coding system would reveal the Crown's approach. Specifically, production of the electronic version of the disclosure "would reveal the approach of the Crown's principal advisers to the way the issues relate in the case and the Crown's strategic interests in the coding would be laid bare." Providing disclosure in electronic form would require the Crown to edit the material to remove its work product and certain other personal information (such as phone numbers, addresses and birth places of witnesses) that was deleted from the hard copies previously provided, and that this task would take approximately three months. The Crown maintained that the issue was not one of disclosure, but rather that the accused was seeking a remedy that would level the playing field.

After weighing the time and effort required, the court concluded that the Crown was not obligated under disclosure principles to delete its work product from the electronic litigation system in order that the defence could receive an electronically identical copy of information that had been completely disclosed in hard copy.[80] However, the defence was permitted to ask the Crown to use its computer in certain circumstances to save the time of the court (such as, when it wished to search for other references when suggesting to a witness that his or her evidence is of recent fabrication).

British Columbia Building Corp. v. T&N plc,[81] involved an application for an order, in part, that a defendant deliver hard copies of documents at its own expense. The

---

78 *Fauteck v. Montgomery Ward & Co., Inc.*, 91 F.R.D. 393 (N.D.Ill., 1980). See also *Hoffman v. United Telecommunications, Inc.*, 117 F.R.D. 436 (D.Kan., 1987). Protection will not be lost if access to the system is only given to experts hired in anticipation of litigation who do not testify at trial.

79 [1997] O.J. No. 924, 24 O.T.C. 266 (Ont. Gen. Div.).

80 However, the court stated that it would have ordered the editing and for the electronic disks to be handed over to the defence if it had concluded that the Crown's possession of the computer disks were to produce an unfair trial. It should also be noted that the court distinguished this case from a situation where the investigating officer had used a computer to record his investigating notes (the court referred to Green, J. in *R. v. Charron* (1996), 443 A.P.R. 170 (Nfld. T.D.).

81 [1995] B.C.J. No. 620 (B.C. S.C.).

defendant had generated approximately one million documents from its worldwide operations that were relevant to the issues raised in the litigation. These were microfilmed and the originals stored in a depository. The court accepted that the cost of reproducing the hard copies of the documents would exceed $250,000, while the microfilm set could be copied for between $9,000 and $15,750. No additional information was contained on the microfilm other than a photograph of those documents that were being made available to the plaintiff. The court did not believe that turning over copies of the microfilm would constitute a "disclosure of the research, investigations and thought processes compiled in the trial brief of opposing counsel" and ordered that such a copy be provided at the cost of the plaintiff. The court commented that it considered the computer retrieval system developed by the defendant for the litigation to be different than the microfilm and that such system would fall into the category of work product. The court also distinguished the case at bar from one where the information being requested included research and investigation of each party's case, as the disclosure of that type of information would give the other party the fruits of the first party's labour and have a negative effect on the adversarial system.

7.8 RESISTING DISCLOSURE

While the disclosure of the electronic forms of evidence is permitted under the rules relating to discovery, such disclosure will not always be ordered by a court, particularly where the costs, burdens, and delays to the party being discovered outweigh the potential usefulness of such discovery. In *Fennell v. First Step Designs, Ltd.*,[82] the plaintiff, who alleged that she had been unlawfully discharged by her employer, sought discovery of the defendant's computer files in the hopes of finding evidence that a particular memo regarding planned layoffs was fabricated after the decision to terminate her had been made. The First Circuit (Court of Appeal) recognized that "there may be cases where discovery of word processing files on a computer hard drive might well be warranted", but that such discovery must be balanced by "the costs, burdens, and delays that the proposed discovery entailed, as well as the likelihood of discovering the evidence of fabrication." Factors that weigh against granting discovery include where:

- the proposed additional discovery would involve "substantial risks and costs" (for instance, as a result of the large quantity of electronic data that might need to be examined);
- the party requesting the disclosure of the electronic evidence had not demonstrated "a particularized likelihood of discovering appropriate information"; or
- the party requesting the disclosure had failed to present a compelling showing that the printed version of the evidence had in fact been fabricated.

---

82   83 F.3d 526 (1st Cir. (Me.), 1996).

A party attempting to resist production may also:

- stipulate to the existence of certain facts;
- argue that the requested material is a trade secret[83] or protected by privilege;
- request all costs associated with extracting and reviewing the requested material prior to disclosure;
- argue that the requested material is not relevant and beyond the scope of what needs to be disclosed;
- raise issues regarding admissibility of the requested material;
- argue that the likelihood of discovering deleted data is low; or
- argue that permitting broad access to their computer system would cause irreparable harm.

7.9 CAVEAT REGARDING ELECTRONIC DISCLOSURE

A party intending to provide an electronic copy of a document to an opponent should ensure that the media being used, such as a floppy diskette, does not contain any deleted files that may still be recoverable by the use of special utility programs, as discussed below. "Used" diskettes may contain recoverable confidential or privileged information. Also, any word processing documents should not have been saved using a "fast save" option because, as previously discussed, this may result in the inclusion of information previously deleted from the on-screen and printed copy of the document.

In the United States, a recommended practice is, therefore, for all parties to expressly agree that inadvertent production of documents does not waive any privilege and that the producing party may request the return of any such documents. If the opposing party disagrees, it may file a motion challenging the substantive privilege claim, but may not assert a theory based on waiver.[84]

---

83 For instance, in *Lawyers Title Ins. Corp. v. U.S. Fidelity & Guar. Co.*, 122 F.R.D. 567 (N.D.Cal., 1988), the court refused to order discovery where there was only a mere possibility of uncovering relevant documents and where there was a risk that the design of a valuable proprietary internal computer system might be misappropriated by a competitor.

84 J.T. Soma & S.G. Austin, "A Practical Guide to Discovering Computerized Files in Complex Litigation", (Review of Litigation, Austin School of Law, University of Texas, Summer 1992). This paper contains some useful checklists for use when either obtaining or avoiding discovery of computerized litigation support systems.

In Canada, inadvertent disclosure of a privileged document is not likely to result in a waiver of privilege and, therefore, there is not a similar need for parties to enter into such an agreement.[85]

7.10 OTHER CONCERNS

In *Derby & Co. Ltd. v. Weldon and others (No 9)*,[86] the court discussed some of the problems that arose in that case and that are likely to occur with increasing frequency in the future:[87]

- Even when the relevant material is on-line and capable of being shown on screen or printed out, some means will have to be found of screening out irrelevant or privileged material. The party seeking discovery cannot be allowed simply to seat himself at his opponent's computer console and be provided with all necessary access keys.
- There may be material on the computer which is not accessible by current programs but which can be retrieved by reprogramming. Prima facie the powers of the court would extend to requiring that the computer be reprogrammed so as to enable the relevant information to be retrieved. Otherwise an unscrupulous litigant would be able to escape discovery by maintaining his records in computerised form and altering current programs when litigation was in prospect so that information previously retrievable could not be retrieved without reprogramming. Of course questions may then arise as to who bears the cost of any necessary reprogramming and whether it can be done without affecting current programs.
- If, as will often be the case, the computer is in daily use, the question may arise—it arose acutely in the instant case—whether access can be arranged, in particular whether any necessary reprogramming can be done or whether information stored in the archival or history files can be retrieved without unduly interrupting the necessary everyday use of the computer.[88]

---

85 For instance, see *Royal Bank v. Lee* (1992), 3 Alta. L.R. (3d) 187, 9 C.P.C. (3d) 199 (Alta. C.A.), and *Anderson Exploration Ltd. v. Pan-Alberta Gas Ltd.* (1998), 61 Alta. L.R. (3d) 38 (Alta. Q.B.), additional reasons at (April 28, 1999), Doc. Calgary 9601-14674 (Alta. Q.B.). However, practically speaking, the game is over once a party inadvertently discloses a smoking gun document.

86 *Supra*, at note 16.

87 *Ibid.*, at 906-907. However, in this case, the experts were able to agree on many of these issues and an agreement was reached between the parties.

88 One of the problems in this case was that the defendant's computer system could only hold two months' restored backup data in addition to the current operational data, and recreating all the backup data would accordingly take a considerable time. Moreover, often when a file has be recreated further time is need to reprogram the system so that current programs can access the recreated data file while continuing to access current files.

- Safeguards may have to be embodied in order to ensure that tapes or discs which may have deteriorated in storage are not damaged by use and that the use of them does not damage the computer's reader. In the instant case, the condition of some discs was such that read once they would be unreadable or only partially readable a second time and the use of some old discs in fact caused damage to the computer's reader.
- In some cases it may be possible for the database to be copied by transfer onto a disc or tape or directly onto another computer. If that is done the material may be capable of being analyzed in ways which were not originally contemplated. Provision may have to be made for the results of any such analysis, any print-outs made, to be made available to the other party in good time so that he is not taken by surprise at the trial.

8

Preservation of Electronic Evidence

8.1 INTRODUCTION

As previously described, when information on a computer system is deleted, most computer systems do not actually erase the information but rather mark, as available for re-use, the storage area that was utilized by the information. The reason for this approach is that the only way a computer can really erase information is to write over it with new information (in the same way that erasing a program stored on a videotape can only be done by recording over it). However, the desire for rapid operation means that this writing over is not performed until new information needs to be stored in the space occupied by the older information that was marked for deletion. Absent the use of special utility programs,[1] the information may actually survive after its apparent deletion. However, this deleted but still recoverable information can be easily and inadvertently destroyed by the continued, day-to-day use of the computer system.

The natural inclination for someone desiring to preserve this information is to make a backup of the entire computer hard disk using commercially available backup software. However, most commercial backup software will *not* copy all the information. Most users of backup software are only interested in copying active files so that they can be restored in the event their primary storage device (*i.e.*, hard disk) becomes inoperative. Therefore, commercial backup programs will not save a copy of deleted files (that may be fully or partially recoverable) or remnants of an older file left in the last storage blocks used by a more recent file.[2] The only way to

---

1 This includes the use of special "WIPE" programs that intentionally overwrite all information contained in unallocated storage locations. A similar effect can be obtained through the use of a disk optimization program, that is used to reorganize the storage of files on a disk so that contiguous storage units are used to store all of the information contained in the same file.

2 This is discussed later in this publication.

preserve the exact state of a computer hard disk properly is either to stop using the computer or make what is known as an "image" or "mirror" copy of the hard disk rather than the more common copying of active files only.

The doctrine of spoliation can result in a court imposing a penalty on a party that destroys or permits the destruction of relevant evidence. The party deprived of the opportunity to examine destroyed evidence could, in cases of jury trials, be entitled to an instruction from the judge to the jury, that the jury could draw an inference that the party that destroyed evidence did so because it could have disclosed facts averse to that party's case. Although the doctrine is more commonly applied for destruction of physical evidence, it may also have application to EMD.

Many litigators and their clients have not been accustomed to thinking about the production of electronic evidence or of taking steps to preserve such evidence even after a lawsuit arises. However, a party that is under an obligation to preserve evidence should immediately identify all sources, including electronic evidence, and take the appropriate action to preserve that evidence. When computer data is collected for evidentiary purposes, the party has a duty to utilize the method that will yield the most complete and accurate results.[3]

8.2 DUTY TO PRESERVE EVIDENCE

(a) Canada

There has generally been little law in Canada on this issue. There is an implication that, once served, parties have an obligation to preserve relevant evidence. However, this obligation may not arise until a party is made aware of a possible claim. In *Farro v. Nutone Electrical Ltd.*,[4] physical evidence was destroyed by the appellants before the respondent had been notified of a possible claim and was therefore unable to inspect the evidence. The Ontario Court of Appeal stated that the plaintiff's failure to preserve the evidence (not due to any failure on the part of the plaintiff) could not provide a successful defence, but did not preclude itself from arriving at an opposite decision given a different set of facts.

Courts generally have some power to deal with the situation where a party destroys relevant evidence. For instance, Rule 30.08(1) of Ontario's *Rules of Civil Procedure* provides that where a party fails to disclose a document in an affidavit of documents or a supplementary affidavit, or fails to produce a document for inspection in compliance with these rules or an order of the court, (a) if the document is favourable to his or her case, the party may not use the document at trial, except

---

3 *Gates Rubber Co. v. Bando Chemical Industries, Ltd.*, 167 F.R.D. 90 (D.Colo., 1996).
4 (1990), 72 O.R. (2d) 637 (Ont. C.A.).

with leave of the trial judge, or (b) if the document is not favourable to his or her case, the court may make such order as is just.[5]

(i) *Spoliation*

It is not clear whether the destruction of evidence gives rise to an independent cause of action in Canadian jurisdictions. One of the earliest decisions of the Supreme Court of Canada to consider spoliation, or the destruction of evidence, was *St. Louis v. R.*[6] The application of the *omnia praesumuntur contra spoliatorem* rule[7] was under consideration in this case. In short, the rule states that if evidence is destroyed, a presumption arises that the evidence destroyed would have been unfavourable to the party who destroyed that evidence. As it is only a presumption, this inference can of course be rebutted.

In *St. Louis*, the appellant supplier brought an action against the Crown to recover the balance alleged to be owing for labour and materials provided pursuant to certain public works contracts. The appellant employed several bookkeepers and assistants to keep track of time sheets, and to prepare pay lists to submit to the government for payment. The Crown refused to pay the total amount of the pay lists, alleging that they were improperly and fraudulently prepared. Unfortunately, the appellant had destroyed the original time books and time sheets relating to the matters in issue.

The court in *St. Louis* held that although the presumption was raised by the appellant's destruction of the original evidence, it was nevertheless rebutted by the *viva voce* testimony of various employees of both the appellant and the Crown. In his judgment, Girouard J. considered the historical origins of the rule and rejected the argument that the destruction of evidence operated as a complete bar to a plaintiff's action/claim:

> The maxim *omnia praesumuntur contra spoliatorem* comes down to us from the Romans who applied it with a good deal of severity, because every business man was supposed to keep regular records of his affairs, at least a ledger or codex; but it is remarkable that the blotter or *Adversaria* had no legal value, not being admissible as evidence in courts of justice, and no one was obliged to keep it beyond one month. If a plaintiff, trader or not, refused to produce his *Codex* or other papers in his possession relating to any claim, his action was rejected purely and simply, the plaintiff being then held to have been guilty of fraud upon the defendant . . . The modern nations, even those governed by

5 See also, *Alberta Rules of Court* 195.
6 (1896), 25 S.C.R. 649 (S.C.C.).
7 This is also sometimes referred to as a "maxim".

the principles of the Roman law, have not been willing to go so far in the application of the maxim, expect in matters of international concern.[8]

It is clear that in Canada, destruction of evidence is not fatal to a party's case, where the destruction was in good faith and without any apparent intention to frustrate the administration of justice. In *Samsonite Canada Inc. v. Enterprises National Dionite Inc.*,[9] the court dismissed the plaintiff's motion to strike out the defendant's statement of defence, as

> such an action on the part of the Court is drastic in that it would remove the capability of the Defendant to defend the action before the Court, and ... the Court is of the opinion that under the circumstances it is not clear how the destruction of this document would justify the Court in striking the statement of defence or any portion thereof as the remedy requested by the Plaintiff in this matter.[10]

In *Dyk v. Protec Automotive Repairs*,[11] the court considered the concept of spoliation in Canadian law, in comparison to the more developed American jurisprudence. The court discussed the American concept of the "spoliation inference" (all things are presumed against a wrongdoer), that is based on the *omnia praesumuntur contra spoliatorem* maxim, and the four requirements for this inference:

1.   the evidence has been destroyed;
2.   the evidence was relevant;
3.   legal proceedings were pending; and
4.   the destruction was an intentional act of the party or the party's agent indicative of fraud or intent to suppress the truth.[12]

The court then reviewed the limited Canadian case law that had considered spoliation and seemed to suggest that the same four factors are required in Canada, and concluded that the inference could not be drawn in the case at bar, as there was no indication "of fraud or an intent to suppress the truth" and there was no "intentional act".

In *Endean v. Canadian Red Cross Society*,[13] the British Columbia Court of Appeal expressly rejected spoliation as a tort in Canadian law, based on the decision in *St.*

---

8   *Ibid.*, at 667.
9   [1995] F.C.J. No. 138 (Fed. T.D.).
10   *Ibid.*, at paragraph 5.
11   (1997), 151 D.L.R. (4th) 374 (B.C. S.C.).
12   S.S. Katz & A.M. Muscaro, "Spoilage of Evidence—Crimes, Sanctions, Inferences and Torts" *Tort & Insurance Law Journal* XXIX:1 (Fall 1993) 61.
13   (1998), 157 D.L.R. (4th) 465 (B.C. C.A.)., leave to appeal to S.C.C. allowed (1998), 235 N.R. 400 (note) (S.C.C.).

Louis v. R. The court interpreted the decision in *St. Louis* as establishing that "spoliation, or the destruction of documents, is an evidentiary rule which raises a presumption —not an independent tort." The court reasoned:

> . . . a rebuttable presumption cannot give rise to a separate and completed tort. The fact of the destruction of evidence is only part of the evidence in the case and standing alone may very well be incomplete. To formulate this as a separate tort may very well be premature in many cases.

> Pushing the application of the maxim *omnia praesumuntur in odium spoliatoris* to the formulation of a tort deprives the defendant of its opportunity to rebut which would otherwise be a rebuttable presumption.[14]

The court in *Endean* further noted that the law as it stands already provides a flexible remedy for victims of destruction of evidence, noting that in some cases expert reports have been excluded[15] and that in others, costs have been denied.[16]

On the other hand, in *Coriale (Litigation Guardian of) v. Sisters of St. Joseph of Sault Ste. Marie,*[17] the Ontario Court (General Division), held that it was not plain and obvious that spoliation could not form the basis of an independent tort. This was an appeal of the decision of Master Peppiatt to allow the plaintiffs to amend their statement of claim and plead the doctrine of spoliation, and to add a claim based on the tort of spoliation. The Ontario Court (General Division) affirmed the decision to allow the doctrine of spoliation to be included in pleadings, being a well-established principle of evidence, as the "amendment proposed by the plaintiffs is, in part, merely a pleading of this principle of evidence."[18]

As to the question of whether the plaintiffs should be allowed to plead a claim based on the tort, the court affirmed the Master's decision to allow the claim to be added. The court did not expressly decide whether or not such a tort could be said to exist in Canadian law, but instead held that the claim should not be dismissed at the pleading stage, it being preferable for such a question to be considered fully at a trial:

> The only real issue is whether the plaintiffs are entitled to plead that the deliberate destruction of evidence by one or more of the defendants can constitute an independent basis for recovery by the plaintiffs. In my view, on

---

14 *Ibid*, at 471.
15 See *Dawes v. Jajcaj* (1995), 15 B.C.L.R. (3d) 240 (B.C. S.C.); *Werner v. Warner Auto-Marine Inc.* (1996), 3 C.P.C. (4th) 110 (Ont. C.A.); *Dyk v. Protec Automobile Repairs, supra,* at note 11.
16 See *Farro v. Nutone Electrical Ltd., supra,* at note 4.
17 (1998), 41 O.R. (3d) 347 (Ont. Gen. Div.).
18 *Ibid*, at 357.

the current state of the law, it cannot be said that such a claim is clearly untenable. It is far from plain and obvious that it *cannot* possibly succeed. Neither is it plain and obvious that spoliation *can* form the basis of an independent tort. This is a novel point of law which has yet to be explored to any extent in Canada and is still in its early stages of development in the United States. It is precisely in this sort of situation that the claim should be permitted to proceed to trial, so that the logic and necessity of such a tort can be tested against the reality of the facts in the case.[19]

(b) United States

There is no general duty on a person to preserve every document in his or her possession. However, there is a duty to preserve relevant evidence, and the courts are prepared to impose sanctions in order to remedy unfair litigation practices and deter abuses in future cases.

The obligation to preserve evidence is an affirmative one. Parties may not destroy crucial evidence simply because a court order was not issued to preserve the evidence.[20] Sanctions may even be imposed if computer records are altered or destroyed in the regular course of business.[21] There may also be an obligation to communicate proper instructions to employees in possession of discoverable materials.[22]

Therefore, legal counsel must instruct clients as to their obligations to preserve potentially relevant evidence when litigation appears likely. As well, clients must be advised to suspend their normal document retention/destruction program with respect to any potentially relevant documents.

---

19 *Ibid*, at 359.
20 *Graves v. Daley*, 526 N.E.2d 679 (Ill.App. 3 Dist., 1988); See also *Stubli v. Big D Intern. Trucks, Inc.*, 810 P.2d 785 (Nev., 1991), where the court followed *Young v. Johnny Ribeiro Bldg., Inc.*, 106 Nev. 88, 787 P.2d 777 (Nev., 1990), and affirmed the trial court's dismissal order which was based on the destruction of important evidence that occurred prior to filing an action and the commencement of discovery. The court in *Stubli* held that the plaintiffs were not free to destroy crucial evidence simply because a court order had not been issued to preserve the evidence.
21 *Wm. T. Thompson Co. v. General Nutrition Corp., Inc.*, 593 F.Supp. 1443 (C.D.Cal., 1984); *National Ass'n of Radiation Survivors v. Turnage*, 115 F.R.D. 543 (N.D.Cal., 1987).
22 *National Ass'n of Radiation Survivors v. Turnage, supra*, at note 21. A federal agency and its attorneys were sanctioned for failing to ensure that the agency preserve a pre-litigation version of its veteran claims database and records of possible claims.

(i) *When Duty Arises*

While it appears clear that the intentional destruction of relevant evidence after a document request has been made, or a subpoena has been served can expose a party to sanctions, it is less clear when the obligation to preserve actually arises. It appears to be accepted that such duty to preserve arises once a party is on notice that documents and information in its possession are relevant to litigation or potential litigation, or are reasonably calculated to lead to the discovery of relevant evidence.[23]

However, it is not always clear when this duty may actually arise in practice. An obligation to preserve evidence has been found to exist:

- once a party has received a discovery request for the particular document;[24]
- for documents likely to be requested in the future in connection with the suit;[25]
- once the initial complaint has been served;[26] and
- before a suit has been initiated, based on
    - notice by the defendant that a suit would be initiated;[27]
    - pre-litigation correspondence that puts a party on notice that the documents are relevant to pending or potential litigation,[28]
    - pre-litigation settlement activities.[29]

Computer Associates Intern., Inc. v. American Fundware, Inc.,[30] involved an action for breach of contract and copyright infringement. Prior to the commencement of the action, the plaintiff had notified the defendant of its concern. This was followed

---

23 *Wm. T. Thompson Co. v. General Nutrition Corp., Inc.*, 593 F.Supp. 1443 (C.D.Cal., 1984), at 1455.

24 *Turner v. Hudson Transit Lines, Inc.*, 142 F.R.D. 68 (S.D.N.Y., 1991), at 72.

25 See indictment of Texaco executives in *U.S. v. Lundwall, infra* at note 38. Also, sanctions may be imposed under FRCP 37(b) even where evidence was destroyed prior to the making of an order for discovery.

26 *Skeete v. McKinsey & Co., Inc.*, 1993 WL 256659 (S.D.N.Y., 1993).

27 In *Capellupo v. FMC Corp.*, 126 F.R.D. 545 (D.Minn., 1989), the court ordered a monetary sanction against a defendant for intentional destruction of documents and other evidence relating to its employment practices that was carried out three months prior to the initiation of a class action employment discrimination suit. However, at least one court has stated that spoliation cannot occur prior to the suit. See *Giant Food Stores Inc. v. Kmart Corp.*, 1996 WL 706586 (E.D.Pa., 1996).

28 *Wm. T. Thompson Co., supra*, at note 23. See also *Capellupo v. FMC Corp.*, 126 F.R.D. 545 (D.Minn., 1989), at 551.

29 In *Computer Associates Intern., Inc. v. American Fundware, Inc.*, 133 F.R.D. 166, 18 U.S.P.Q.2d 1649, Copy. L. Rep. (CCH) P26,685 (D.Colo., 1990), the defendant was sanctioned for failing to preserve older versions of source code, that were destroyed prior to filing of a suit, because it knew of the plaintiff's copyright infringement claims relating to the software while the parties were attempting to settle their differences.

30 *Ibid.*

with a meeting between the parties that failed to resolve the dispute. Only then did the plaintiff file the action.

It had been the defendant's practice, that the court found was commonly followed in the industry, to only retain the then current version of the source code for its software.[31] That is, as the computer program was revised, previous versions were destroyed. A few months after filing the complaint, the plaintiff served a production request on the defendant seeking the source code for the defendant's program. This was followed with a motion to compel discovery of the source code. The defendant continued with its practice of destroying older versions of the source code for approximately four months after the motion to compel was filed.

The plaintiff argued that once the defendant knew, or should have known, that the source code probably would be critical evidence in pending or imminent litigation, a duty arose to preserve it. The court found that it was:

> ... inconceivable that after the [initial meeting between the parties], [the defendant] did not realize that the software in its possession would be sought through discovery. Certainly commencement of the action settled any doubts. Thereafter the request for production, followed by the motion to compel, provided repeated, insistent reminders of the duty to preserve this irreplaceable evidence. Yet the destruction proceeded.

The court found that even if it gave the defendant the benefit of every doubt, the defendant was subject to a duty to preserve the source code no later than the due date for it to file an answer to the complaint (20 days after filing). Any destruction after such date could not be excused as *bona fide* business practice, and therefore such practice was intentional and an intentional violation of discovery obligations.

(ii) *Sanctions*

Sanctions[32] for failing to preserve may include:

- an adverse inference instruction;[33]

---

31 For another case involving the destruction of source code, see *Cabnetware v. Sullivan*, No. S-90-0313 (E.D. Cal. July 15, 1991).

32 See also Kirby & Steele, "Consequences of Document Destruction in Commercial Litigation", in Gorelick *et al.*, *Destruction of Evidence* (1989 & Supp. 1995).

33 A party that destroys relevant evidence, even if not directly punished by the court, assumes the risk that its action will generate a presumption in the minds of the trier of fact that the evidence was destroyed because its production would have been against the interest of that party. In *Computer Associates Intern., Inc. v. American Fundware, Inc.*, *supra*, at note 29, the court stated "[i]t is familiar doctrine that if a party fails to

- sanctions under discovery rules, including:[34]
  - contempt sanctions,
  - monetary sanctions,[35]
  - deeming of designated facts,
  - preclusion of offending party from supporting or opposing designated claims or defences,
  - prohibiting the introduction of designated matters into evidence,
  - precluding testimony from an expert witness,[36]
  - striking part or all of the pleadings,
  - dismissing part or all of the action, and
  - granting a default judgment against the offending party;[37]

---

produce from within its control evidence that is relevant and material, the fair inference is that that evidence would have weighed against the party who held it back. *A fortiori*, where a party destroys evidence after being put on notice that it is important to a lawsuit, and being placed under a legal obligation to preserve and produce it, the compelling inference is that the evidence would have supported the opposing party's case."

A court may allow an instruction to the jury that it may infer the evidence destroyed or rendered unavailable was adverse to the position of the party that destroyed it. For instance, see *Calif. Evidence Code* Sec. 413, that provides "In determining what inferences to draw from the evidence or facts in the case against a party, the trier of fact may consider, among other things, the party's ... wilful suppression of evidence relating thereto". In the case of negligent destruction of evidence, a nexus may need to be established between the information contained in the destroyed evidence and the requested inference instruction. Such nexus may not need to be established if the evidence is destroyed in bad faith.

34 For instance, see *Calif. Code of Civil Procedure*, section 2023.

35 See *In re Prudential Ins. Co. of America Sales Practises Litigation*, 169 F.R.D. 598 (D.N.J., 1997), where the court imposed a sanction of $1 million plus reimbursement of the plaintiff's attorney fees (it should be noted that wilful misconduct was not found in this case). See also *In re E.I. DuPont De Nemours & Company—Benlate Litigation*, 99 F.3d 363 (11th Cir. (Ga.), 1996), *certiorari* denied by *duPont de Nemours and Co. v. Bush Ranch Inc.*, 118 S.Ct. 263, (U.S., 1997) where sanctions of almost $14 million were imposed (reversed on procedural grounds). Monetary sanctions may be based on the opposing party's legal fees for the additional discovery efforts necessitated by the destruction of evidence, and may be a multiple of such costs to serve as a deterrent. See also Wm. T. Thompson, *supra*, that included an award of $457,000 in attorney fees.

36 For instance, where electronic data used in modelling certain systems in preparation for rendering of an opinion at trial were not retained. See *Hughes Aircraft Co. v. Century Indem. Co.*, 141 F.3d 1176 (9th Cir. (Cal.), 1998).

37 Reckless or intentional destruction of relevant evidence can even potentially lead to a default judgement for the other party—see *Computer Associates Intern. Inc., v. American Fundware, Inc., supra.*, at note 29. For a case not specific to electronic evidence, see *Carlucci v. Piper Aircraft Corp.* where the court entered a default judgement against the defendant after finding that it had a program of destroying all documents that might potentially be harmful in a lawsuit.

- disciplinary sanctions against attorneys who participate in the spoliation; and
- criminal prosecution (in serious cases).[38]

A number of courts have examined the circumstances where a sanction amounting to dismissal or default judgment might be appropriate.

In *Young v. Johnny Ribeiro Bldg., Inc.*,[39] the Supreme Court of Nevada set out a non-exhaustive list of factors that a court may properly consider in deciding whether dismissal is an appropriate sanction. The factors include:

- the degree of wilfulness of the offending party;
- the extent to which the non-offending party would be prejudiced by a lesser sanction;
- the severity of the sanction of dismissal relative to the severity of the discovery abuse;
- whether any evidence has been irreparably lost;
- the policy favouring adjudication on the merits;
- whether any sanctions unfairly operate to penalize a party for the misconduct of his or her attorney; and
- the need to deter both the parties and future litigants from similar abuses.

In *Computer Associates Intern., Inc. v. American Fundware, Inc.*,[40] the court granted the plaintiff's request for default judgment as the appropriate sanction. In imposing this sanction, the court acknowledged that it is one of the most severe sanctions available and is reserved for egregious offences against an opposing party or the court. It stated that default judgment should be considered, as a last resort to be invoked only if no lesser, yet equally effective, sanction is available. Employing default as a sanction may require finding that:

- the responding party acted willfully or in bad faith;
- the requesting party was seriously prejudiced by the responding party's conduct; and
- alternative sanctions would not adequately punish the responding party or deter future discovery violations.[41]

---

38 For instance, Texaco executives were indicted for destroying documents after describing them at a deposition in order to avoid producing them in a civil suit. See *U.S. v. Lundwall*, 1 F.Supp. 2d 249 (S.D.N.Y., 1998). See also *Calif. Penal Code* section 135 that provides "Every person who, knowing that any book, paper, record, instrument in writing, or other matter or thing, is about to be produced in evidence upon any trial, inquiry, or investigation whatever, authorized by law, willfully destroys or conceals same, with intent thereby to prevent it from being produced, is guilty of a misdemeanor."

39 106 Nev. 88, 787 P.2d 777 (Nev., 1990).

40 *Supra*, at note 29.

41 Citing *Telectron, Inc. v. Overhead Door Corp.*, 116 F.R.D. 107 (S.D.Fla., 1987), at 130.

The court found that "destroying the best evidence relating to the core issue in the case inflicts the ultimate prejudice upon the opposing party." It concluded by stating:

> In this post Iran-gate era of widely publicized evidence destruction by document shredding, it is well to remind litigants that such conduct will not be tolerated in judicial proceedings. Destruction of evidence cannot be countenanced in a justice system whose goal is to find the truth through honest and orderly production of evidence under established discovery rules.

In circumstances where the destruction of evidence occurred due to negligence, sanctions of dismissal or default judgement are not likely to be imposed. The more likely sanctions will be those of an adverse inference or a monetary award.

(iii) *Authority to Impose Sanctions*

The court's authority to impose sanctions arises from a number of sources:

- federal obstruction of justice legislation;[42]
- *Federal Rules of Civil Procedure*;[43]
- the presiding court's "inherent authority" to regulate litigation, preserve and protect the integrity of the proceedings before it and sanction parties for abusive practices;[44]
- spoliation as tortious conduct.[45]

---

42 18 U.S.C. 1503 (1984) or similar statutes enacted in many states. This was the basis for the imposition of criminal liability in the *Texaco* case.

43 It is not clear whether such authority is limited to the concealment or destruction of documents that violates a specific order of the court or whether a party that destroys documents prior to a document request can be sanctioned because its inability to comply was self-inflicted. See also *FRCP 37*.

44 *Capellupo v. FMC Corp.*, 126 F.R.D. 545 (D.Minn., 1989) at 551 citing *Roadway Exp., Inc. v. Piper*, 447 U.S. 752, 100 S.Ct. 2455 (U.S.La., 1980). However, this may require a particularized showing of (i) bad faith; (ii) abusive litigation practices; or (iii) destruction that is brought about "in bad faith, vexatiously, wantonly, or for oppressive reasons." See *Turner v. Hudson Transit Lines, Inc.*, 142 F.R.D. 68 (S.D.N.Y., 1991). See also R.F. Ziegler & S.A. Stuhl, "Spoliation Issues Arise in Digital Era" *The National Law Journal* (16 February 1998) B09.

45 Some states recognize spoliation as tortious conduct that can give rise to an action for damages. Some have limited this tort to intentional destruction, while others have permitted recovery for even negligent destruction.

(iv) *Spoliation as Tortious Conduct*

Spoliation is destruction or significant alteration of evidence, or failure to preserve property for another's use as evidence, in pending or future litigation.[46]

A number of US states have recognized an independent cause of action in tort for intentional or negligent spoliation of evidence.[47] Some courts have declined to adopt this cause of action, either in general, or on the facts of a particular case.[48] In *Cedars-Sinai Medical Center v. Superior Court*,[49] the California Supreme Court rejected prior California lower court decisions that had recognized this tort.

Common elements of the tort of spoliation (that may vary from state to state) include:[50]

- pending or probable civil litigation;
- defendant's knowledge that litigation is pending or probable;
- willful destruction of evidence;
- intent to interfere with plaintiff's prospective civil suit;
- a causal relationship between the evidence destroyed and the inability to prove the lawsuit; and
- damages.

8.3 AFFIDAVIT OF DOCUMENTS

In some jurisdictions, parties are required to produce a list of all relevant documents, including documents no longer in a party's possession, within certain

46 *Willard v. Caterpillar, Inc.*, 40 Cal.App.4th 892, 48 Cal.Rptr.2d 607 (Cal.App. 5 Dist., 1995), at 616 citing other sources.
47 See D.J. Vendler, "Court Nixes Spoliation As a Tort" *The National Law Journal* (20 July 1998) B07, citing *Smith v. Howard Johnson Co. Inc.*, 615 N.E.2d 1037 (Ohio, 1993); *Hazen v. Municipality of Anchorage*, 718 P.2d 456 (Alaska, 1986); *Bondu v. Gurvich*, 473 So.2d 1307 (Fla.App. 3 Dist., 1984), review denied by *Cedars of Lebanon Hosp. Care Center, Inc. v. Bondu*, 484 So.2d 7 (Fla., 1986). See also Ballon, *supra*, listing Alaska, Florida, Kansas and California (but see *Cedars-Sinai, infra*); See also Rowse, "Spoliation: Civil Liability for Destruction of Evidence" (1985), 20 *U. Rich. L. Rev.* 191.
48 See Vendler, *supra*, citing *La Raia v. Superior Court In and For Maricopa County*, 722 P.2d 286 (Ariz., 1986); *Gardner v. Blackston*, 365 S.E.2d 545 (Ga.App., 1988); *Koplin v. Rosel Well Perforators Inc.*, 734 P.2d 1177 (Kan., 1987). See also *Ballon, supra*, listing Georgia, the District of Columbia, Maryland, Missouri and New York as jurisdictions that have declined to do so.
49 98 Daily Journal D.A.R. 4881 (Cal., 1998).
50 Ballon, *supra*.

specified time periods. Business entities that have not properly organized their electronic data may have trouble meeting such requirements.

(a) Ontario

In Ontario, Rule 30.03(1) of the *Rules of Civil Procedure* provides that each party is required to serve an affidavit of documents within 10 days of the close of pleadings.[51] The affidavit is to list and describe documents that are in the party's possession, control or power and that the party does not object to producing, documents no longer in a party's possession and documents in respect of which a claim of privilege is made.[52]

The affidavit must state that the party has never had possession, control or power over any document relating to the matter in issue in the action other than those listed in the affidavit. In addition, in order to ensure that the party understands the broad scope of discovery, the party's solicitor is required to endorse on the affidavit a certificate that he or she has explained to the deponent the necessity of making full disclosure of all relevant documents.[53]

These obligations are ongoing—if a party later comes into possession of a document related to a matter in issue in the action or discovers that the affidavit is inaccurate or incomplete, then that party must provide a supplementary affidavit and disclose any additional documents.[54]

A party that fails to comply with these disclosure obligations could be subject to serious sanctions. A wide discretion is granted to the court to sanction where a party's rights to discovery have been prejudiced. In Ontario, a court has the power to dismiss the action if the party is a plaintiff, or to strike out the statement of defence if the party is a defendant, or to make such other order as is just.[55]

---

51 The party must disclose to the full extent of their knowledge, information and belief all documents relating to any matter in issue in the action that are or have been in the party's possession, control or power. *Alberta Rules of Court* Rule 186(2) provides that any time after the close of pleadings a party may serve any other party adverse in interest with a Notice to Produce. The recipient of such notice is required to file and serve the party who delivered the Notice with an affidavit of documents within 10 days of receipt of that Notice. It is common practice to grant extensions of the period for response.

52 Rule 30.03(2) of the *Rules of Civil Procedure*. See also Rule 188 of the *Alberta Rules of Court*.

53 Rule 30.03(4) of the *Rules of Civil Procedure*.

54 Rule 30.07 of the *Rules of Civil Procedure*. See also Rule 195(1) of the *Alberta Rules of Court*. In addition, Alberta Rule 703(b) provides that a person who fails to comply with any notice or order served upon him for production of documents within his power or possession is in civil contempt.

55 Rule 30.08(2) of the *Rules of Civil Procedure*. See also Rule 195(2) of the *Alberta Rules of Court*. In addition, Alberta Rule 703(b) provides that a person who fails to comply

(b) United States

Similar obligations apply to US litigants. *Federal Rule of Civil Procedure* 26(a) requires parties to exchange lists of relevant electronic data, as well as paper documents, early in the litigation process (within approximately three months after litigation commences). Rule 26(a)(1) provides:

> Except to the extent otherwise stipulated or directed by order or local rule, a party shall, without awaiting a discovery request, provide to other parties . . . (B) a copy of, or a description by category and location of, all . . . data compilations . . . in the possession, custody or control of the party that are relevant to the disputed facts alleged with particularity in the proceedings.

There is also a corresponding requirement in *Federal Rule of Civil Procedure* 26(g) that "the lawyer has made a reasonable effort to assure that the client has provided all the information and documents available to him that are responsive to the discovery demand."

Failure to produce a list of all relevant electronic data may impact a defendant's case further down the road, if, for instance, exculpatory evidence is later discovered. Such evidence may be subject to attack as having been fabricated, due to its exclusion from such lists. If such exculpatory evidence is discovered after substantial discovery has already taken place there is a risk that such evidence may be excluded or alternatively, the defendant may be required to pay certain costs associated with the discovery. If damaging evidence is later discovered the plaintiff may seek to portray the defendant as having engaged in a cover up.

8.4 STATUTORY RECORD KEEPING OBLIGATIONS

A duty to preserve evidence or records, including those in electronic form, also arises from various record keeping requirements imposed on individuals and businesses by federal and provincial/state laws of general application.[56] The required retention period will vary depending on the type of records and the legislation in question.

---

with any notice or order for production of documents, within his power or possession, served upon him, is in civil contempt.

56 See the discussion regarding *Armstrong v. Executive Office of the President* in section 1.1(a) of this publication.

8.5 SUMMARY AND CONCLUSIONS

A party seeking production of electronic evidence in a civil action or a government investigation should consider providing the other party with sufficient notice of possible sources of electronic evidence, and its duty to preserve, so that the other party will not be able to claim later that the evidence was destroyed because it lacked knowledge of such evidence. The other party and its counsel may be unaware of these potentially hidden sources of information and the ease with which they can be destroyed. They may need to be educated about their existence so that appropriate action can be taken to preserve these sources.

If counsel has reason to believe that the opposing party is in possession of relevant evidence, including electronic evidence, and is likely, purposely or inadvertently, to destroy such evidence, counsel can seek an interim order for preservation.[57] Such an order could provide for an independent computer expert to capture a proper backup of the opposing party's computer systems.

A client may need to be advised to take proper action to preserve the relevant evidence it has in electronic form. It is important to stress that action must be taken in the early phases of the proceeding because mere routine use of the computer system can lead to the destruction of such potential evidence.

---

57 For example, see Rule 45.01(1) of the *Rules of Civil Procedure*. See also Rule 468 of the *Alberta Rules of Court*.

9

Admissibility of Electronic Evidence at Trial

9.1 INTRODUCTION

Other chapters have provided information on how to find electronic evidence, and on obligations relating to preservation and disclosure. This chapter will review the general issues surrounding the admissibility and use of such evidence at trial, particularly computer-produced evidence. The intent is not to provide a comprehensive tutorial on the topic of admissibility, but rather to highlight some of the issues particularly relevant to computer-produced evidence.[1]

It is now settled law in many jurisdictions that computer-produced evidence, in the form of a computer printout, is admissible as evidence at trial. Given the reliance by our society on electronics generally, and computers in particular, matters of proof in litigation would be greatly hindered without the benefit of the admission of such evidence. For instance, in *Tecoglas Inc. v. Domglas Inc.*,[2] the court made the following observations about the prevalence of computers, while admitting computer printouts as evidence:

> There are not many large enterprises operating successfully today who do not use computers in connection with their record-keeping. It would be almost impossible and certainly impractical to prove expenditures of the nature of those in this case without admitting the computer records or documents based on the computer print-out.[3]

---

1   It should also be noted that the rules of evidence differ from jurisdiction to jurisdiction, and any references to legislation or case law cited in this chapter are included for illustrative purposes. They are not intended to be a complete or conclusive summary of the applicable issues.

2   (1985), 51 O.R. (2d) 196 (Ont. H.C.).

3   *Ibid*, at 205.

Similarly, in *R. v. Minors*,[4] the UK Court of Appeal noted:

> The law of evidence must be adapted to the realities of contemporary business practice. Mainframe computers, minicomputers and microcomputers play a pervasive role in our society. Often the only record of a transaction, which nobody can be expected to remember, will be in the memory of a computer. The versatility, power and frequency of use of computers will increase. If computer output cannot relatively readily be used as evidence in criminal cases, much crime (and notably offences involving dishonesty) will in practice be immune from prosecution.

The biggest challenge to the use of computer-produced data as evidence at trial is that it does not fall comfortably within the traditional classifications of evidence.[5] Part of the problem may be that computer-produced evidence may include:

- documentary evidence which originates from a person, and where the computer is primarily being used as an electronic filing cabinet;
- electronic data corresponding to events monitored and recorded by the computer without human intervention (for instance, long distance telephone calls made by hotel guests); and
- data generated by the computer where the computer is used to interpret or analyze data supplied directly by external sensors (such as a breathalizer or a radar speed gun).

Each of these may raise different issues for a litigator trying to decide how to lay the foundation for admission of such computer-produced evidence, or trying to prevent the opposing party from using such information.

9.2 REAL EVIDENCE v. DOCUMENTARY EVIDENCE

Most jurisdictions have accepted that electronic data stored inside a computer system may constitute a "document",[6] and that the rules of documentary evidence

---

4 [1989] 2 All E.R. 208 (Eng. C.A.).

5 There are three general types of evidence: (i) *Testimonial/Oral*, also called *"viva voce"* evidence, is evidence given by a witness to the fact in issue; (ii) *Real/Physical* evidence is a type of evidence which may be appreciated by the senses; and (iii) *Documentary* or paper evidence is essentially evidence comprised of "documents" or "records".

6 The definitions of "document" found in the rules of court for most jurisdictions are generally broad enough to include many forms of electronic evidence. For instance, Rule 30.01(1)(a) of the *Rules of Civil Procedure* (Ontario) provides that "document" includes a sound recording, videotape, film, photograph, chart, graph, amp, plan, survey, book of account and information recorded or stored by means of any device. [R.R.O. 1990, Regulation 194.]. See also Rule 337 of the *Alberta Rules of Court*.

govern its admissibility.[7] Specifically, the principles applicable to *business* records will generally govern records kept by computer systems.[8]

If admission of electronic evidence is sought on the basis of it being a "document", issues concerning the application of the following rules of evidence to electronic evidence are raised: (i) hearsay, (ii) the best evidence rule, and (iii) authentication. It may also be necessary to consider whether the electronic evidence fits under applicable definitions of "original", "record" or "copy".

The specific rules of evidence that pertain to documents only apply where the contents of the document are sought to be proved as true, through the admission of the document alone. There may be instances when the electronic data itself may not be needed to prove the truth of the data at trial, but may be used only to prove the existence of the data, or its possession in the hands of a certain party. That is, the computer evidence is relied on *circumstantially* rather than *testimonially*. In such cases, the data from a computer can be classified as real evidence, and not documentary evidence.[9] For example, a computer hard drive that contains images of child pornography may be introduced merely to prove it was in the accused's possession.[10]

Real evidence usually takes the form of some material object (including computer output) produced for inspection in order that the court may draw an inference from its own observation as to the existence, condition or value of the object in question. Although real evidence may be extremely valuable as a means of proof, little if any weight attaches to it unless accompanied by testimony which identifies the object in question and explains its connection with, or significance in relation to, the facts in issue or relevant to the issue.[11]

---

7 See K. Chasse, "Computer-Produced Records in Court Proceedings" *Uniform Law Conference of Canada*; J.D. Ewart, *Documentary Evidence in Canada* (Toronto: Carswell, 1984) at 16-18.

8 See J. Sopinka, S. N. Lederman & A. W. Bryant, *The Law of Evidence in Canada* (Toronto: Butterworths, 1992) at 214:

Computer printouts are now a part of everyday life. Such methods of record-keeping were not contemplated when the business records legislation was originated. Accordingly, in the absence of special legislation to deal specifically with computer records, it would appear that the courts will apply principles to this type of record analogous to those they apply to general business documents.

9 See *R. v. Spilby* (1990), 91 Cr. App. R. 186, [1991] C.R. L.R. 199 (Eng. C.A.); *R. v. Minors*, *supra*, at note 4.

10 Another issue in respect of computer-based evidence is whether certain audible or visual content stored in electronic format, which cannot be seen or heard without the use of computer equipment, retain certain characteristics. In *U.S. v. Hockings*, 129 F.3d 1069 (9th Cir., (Cal.), 1997), pornographic images of children stored electronically in graphic image format (GIF) were found to be "visual depictions" under federal child pornography legislation.

11 A. Hoey, "Analysis of The Police and Criminal Evidence Act, s. 69—Computer Generated Evidence" (1996) 1 Web Journal of Current Legal Issues.

9.3 THE RULE AGAINST HEARSAY

(a) Introduction

Ideally, evidence at trial should be in the form of a sworn oral account of facts—it should be the testimony of a witness who has *personal knowledge* of the facts being presented. This is generally considered the best type of evidence. In addition to having personal knowledge of the subject matter, the witness should be available in person at trial, to have his account of the facts tested through cross-examination by the opposing party.

An out of court statement made to the witness who is testifying is hearsay if the object of offering the evidence is to establish the truth of what is contained in the statement.[12] As a general rule, hearsay evidence is inadmissible. However, the evidence *is not* hearsay and *is* admissible when the object of offering the evidence is merely to establish the fact that the statement was made.

The exclusionary effects of the hearsay rule can make some matters of proof extremely difficult, especially with electronic evidence, where computer data is often not entered by a person with personal knowledge of the matters. Also, the person presenting the information contained in electronic documents as evidence in court will usually not have personal knowledge of that information.[13]

Due to the necessity of introducing hearsay evidence in many situations, numerous exceptions and qualifications to the hearsay rule have developed. In a number of jurisdictions, hearsay evidence can now be said to be admissible as long as it is shown to be reliable and its admission is necessary to the proper adjudication of the case.[14] One of the more common exceptions is that provided for business records.

(b) Exceptions—Business Records

An important exception to the hearsay rule, in respect of computer-produced evidence, is the exception for business records. The composition of the business

---

12 In the United States, *Federal Rule of Evidence* 801(c) defines hearsay as a statement, other than one made by a declarant while testifying at the trial or hearing, offered in evidence to prove the truth of the matter asserted.

13 J. D. Gregory & E. Tollefson, "Proposals for a Uniform Electronic Evidence Act" (1995).

14 *Ibid.*

records exception varies slightly from jurisdiction to jurisdiction, but generally shares a number of the following conditions, which provide a circumstantial guarantee of accuracy and truth:

- made by persons (at common law, these had to be deceased at the time of trial);
- contemporaneously with personal knowledge of the matters being recorded;
- in the ordinary course of business;
- as a result of a duty to perform an act and/or to record it; and
- where there was no motive to misrepresent.

In *U.S. v. Snyder*[15] the court stated:

> The business records exception is based on a presumption of accuracy, accorded because the information is part of a regularly conducted activity, kept by those trained in the habits of precision, and customarily checked for correctness, and because of the accuracy demanded in the conduct of the nation's business.

(i) *Common Law Exceptions*

An exception to the hearsay rule developed at common law for business records. This exception made admissible statements made by a deceased person, who was under a duty to another to do an act and to record the act, in the ordinary course of the deceased declarant's business.[16]

Admitting hearsay evidence under these circumstances was *necessary*, as the declarant was now dead. Such evidence was also *reliable*, as the record had been made by a declarant who was under a duty to record to his employer, and was faced with the fear of discipline and dismissal if he breached his duty.

A leading Canadian case which broadened the business records exception was the decision of the Supreme Court of Canada in *Ares v. Venner*.[17] In that case, the court held that the criteria that judges should follow in restating exceptions to the hearsay

---

15 787 F.2d 1429 (10th Cir. (Kan.), 1986) *certiorari* denied by, 479 U.S. 836 (U.S.Kan., 1986) at 1432, 1433.

16 See Sopinka, *supra*, at 187. J.D. Ewart, "Documentary Evidence: The Admissibility of Documents Under Section 30 of the Canada Evidence Act" (1979-1980), 22 C.L.Q. 189 at 913, summarized the requirements to be met for the business records exception as follows: the record had to be (i) an original entry; (ii) made contemporaneously with the event recorded, (iii) in the routine, (iv) of business, (v) by a person since deceased, (vi) who was under a specific duty to another to do the very thing and record it, and (vii) who had no motive to misrepresent.

17 [1970] S.C.R. 608 (S.C.C.).

rule are the principles of *necessity* and *circumstantial guarantees of trustworthiness.*[18]

Some specific requirements for admission of hospital records were set out by the Court in *Ares*. It was held that the records must have been made:

- in the regular and routine course of work;
- contemporaneously;
- by a person with personal knowledge;
- by a person whose duty it was to observe and record; and
- by a person who is available for cross-examination.[19]

Although the admission of hospital records was under consideration in *Ares*, later decisions have indicated that this new broad exception applies to all types of business records.[20] In *Tecoglas Inc. v. Domglas Inc.*[21] the court interpreted *Ares v. Venner* more broadly, to allow the admissibility of evidence without the personal knowledge of the recorder, if there is necessity and the circumstances in which it was prepared provide a reasonable guarantee of reliability or trustworthiness.

The trend in Canada has been to admit hearsay where it can be shown to be necessary and reliable. With respect to computer-produced data, this "principled approach" may emphasize the need to demonstrate the reliability of the relevant computer system.[22] As Ewart has observed in *Documentary Evidence in Canada*:

> As Wigmore [Wigmore on Evidence] so carefully shows, most of the exceptions to the hearsay rule which have been created over several centuries can be found to have been constructed on two fundamental principles: necessity, and a circumstantial guarantee of trustworthiness. Of these two fundamental standards, the second is by far the more compelling; a court can feel relatively comfortable in breaking new ground if it has been satisfied that the circumstances of the document's creation provide an adequate substitute for the traditional safeguard of cross-examination. The proponent of a document should seek to persuade the court that the document, *because of the circumstances of its creation*, is inherently reliable. If this is done, then the necessity doctrine can likely be satisfied by demonstrating that there is not [*sic*] other equally convenient way to put before the court the information in question.[23]

---

18 The principles of necessity and circumstantial guarantees of trustworthiness were taken from Wigmore, *infra*.

19 *Ares, supra*, at 626. It is unclear whether the declarant's availability for cross-examination is actually a requirement for admissibility or just a matter going to weight.

20 See *Setak Computer Services Corp. v. Burroughs Business Machines Ltd.* (1977), 15 O.R. (2d) 750 (Ont. H.C.).

21 *Supra*, at note 2.

22 H. Stewart, "Some Thoughts on Computer-Generated Evidence" (1996).

23 J.D. Ewart, *Documentary Evidence in Canada* (Toronto: Carswell, 1984) at 13.

In Canada, two frequently cited cases dealing with computer-produced evidence involve interpretation of section 29 of the *Canada Evidence Act*.[24] In *R. v. McMullen*,[25] the Crown sought to introduce a computer printout of an accused's bank account. The trial judge held that the computer's memory was not a "record" and therefore the printout was not admissible under section 29 as a copy of a record. This interpretation was rejected by the Court of Appeal, which held that "record" should be read broadly. However, the Court of Appeal suggested that the proponent of a computer-produced document must provide detailed foundation evidence as a pre-condition of admission:

> The nature and quality of the evidence put before the Court has to reflect the facts of the complete record keeping process—in the case of computer records, the procedures and processes relating to the input of entries, storage of information, and its retrieval and presentation . . .

The Court acknowledged that proving the reliability of computer evidence is a more complex process than proving the reliability of written records and stated that as a matter of principle, a court should carefully scrutinize the foundation put before it to support a finding of reliability, as a condition of admissibility.

In a subsequent case, *R. v. Bell*,[26] the Court interpreted *R. v. McMullen* as holding that information stored in a computer is *capable* of being a "record kept in a financial institution" and that a corresponding computer printout is *capable* of being a copy of that record. However, in *R. v. Bell*, the Court held that it was also possible for the printout itself to be the "record". In admitting the printouts, the Court emphasized the record keeper's reliance on the record as opposed to the operation of the relevant computer system. The Court seemed content to take the bank's reliance on its own system as a substitute for the more detailed inquiry into the manner in which the information underlying the printout was recorded and processed, as contemplated by *R. v. McMullen*.[27]

In the United States, the common law exception to the hearsay rule for business records, also known as the *shopbook rule*, has also been expanded to accommodate modern business practices.[28] For instance, in *King v. State for Use and Benefit of*

---

24 Although this provision deals with records of federally regulated financial institutions, the reasoning in these cases may provide guidance in respect of records of other businesses.

25 (1978), 42 C.C.C. (2d) 67 (Ont. H.C.), affirmed (1979), 47 C.C.C. (2d) 499 (Ont. C.A.).

26 (1982), 35 O.R. (2d) 164 (Ont. C.A.), affirmed (sub nom. *Bruce v. R.*) [1985] 2 S.C.R. 287 (S.C.C.).

27 These two cases are discussed in more detail in the next section, which deals with the best evidence rule.

28 For instance, to omit the requirement for personal knowledge where it would be inconvenient to call the originators of the records.

Murdock Acceptance Corp.[29] the Supreme Court of Mississippi held that computer printouts were admissible as evidence where it would be *inconvenient* to call at trial the individual makers of the records from which the permanent record was compiled. The following conditions for admissibility were given by the Court:

- the electronic equipment is recognized as standard equipment;
- the entries were made in the normal course of business at, or reasonably near, the time the event occurred; and
- there is foundation testimony that satisfies the court of the reliability of the sources of information, and the method and time of preparation.[30]

(ii) *Statutory Exceptions*

In a number of jurisdictions, the common law exemptions for business records in general, or computer-produced evidence in particular, have been supplemented[31] or replaced by legislation. The *Canada Evidence Act*[32] applies to the admissibility of records in proceedings under federal jurisdiction (including criminal prosecutions). Otherwise, the relevant provincial Evidence Act will be applicable. Computer-based data appears to fall within the definitions of business records of both the federal and the various provincial Evidence Acts.

In Ontario, the circumstances of the making of a record, including lack of knowledge by the maker, can affect the weight to be given to the evidence but not its admissibility. Also, under both federal and provincial legislation, proof that there is no motive to misrepresent now goes to weight to be given to the evidence rather than its admissibility.

Legislation in the United States has also relaxed the requirements necessary to admit business records.

(A) *Canada Evidence Act*

The *Canada Evidence Act*[33] provides a statutory exception to the hearsay rule for *original* business "records". Subsection 30(1) provides as follows:

---

29 222 So.2d 393 (Miss., 1969).

30 As discussed in R. MacKinnon, "Admissibility of Computer-Produced Evidence", CBAO, Young Lawyers' Division—Basic Evidence (2 November 1991).

31 Evidence may be admissible under the common law exception even if it does not meet the requirements of the legislation (which are generally easier to meet but may not be for a particular set of circumstances).

32 R.S.C. 1985, c. C-5.

33 *Ibid.*

Where oral evidence in respect of a matter would be admissible in a legal proceeding, a record made in the usual and ordinary course of business that contains information in respect of that matter is admissible in evidence under this section in the legal proceeding on production of the record.

Both "business" and "record" are broadly defined in this section:

"business" means any business, profession, trade, calling, manufacture or undertaking of any kind carried on in Canada or elsewhere whether for profit or otherwise, including any activity or operation carried on or performed in Canada or elsewhere by any government, by any department, branch, board, commission or agency of any government, by any court or other tribunal or by any other body or authority performing a function of government.[34]

"record" includes the whole or any part of any book, document, paper, card, tape or other thing on or in which information is written, recorded, stored or reproduced . . .[35]

It is not necessary that the actual maker of the record appear in person as a foundation witness. However, it is advisable to enter the records through the evidence of a witness who has had custody of the records and is able to identify them as records made in the usual and ordinary course of business. This witness should also be able to describe the usual and ordinary course of business under which the records were made and kept.[36]

Section 30 of the *Canada Evidence Act* seems to impose no preconditions to admissibility, apart from being a record made in the usual and ordinary course of business and relating to a matter in respect of which oral evidence would be admissible. However, subsection 30(6) allows for the court to consider foundation evidence in determining the admissibility and/or weight of the evidence.

In *R. v. Shephard*[37] the court held that meeting the criteria of section 30 did not guarantee admission in every case and that the reliability of the record would have

---

34 *Ibid.*, subsection 30(12).

35 *Ibid.*

36 See *R. v. Grimba* (1977), 38 C.C.C. (2d) 469 (Ont. Co. Ct.). In response to a challenge by defence counsel that the Crown's foundation witness should not be allowed to testify, as he was not the maker of the documents, Callaghan Co. Ct. J. held (at 473):

It goes without saying that Mr. Harper of course has no knowledge of the making of the documents, but in my view, it was intended that any person in an official position such as he, with an agency that maintains a record of such documents in the ordinary course of its business, would have the knowledge of the contents of those documents based on his experience in that business . . .

37 *Infra.*

to be considered. In *R. v. Rowbotham*, admission of computer printouts of telephone bills was refused for various reasons, one of them being that, while:

> . . . the documents may be admissible pursuant to section 30 of the *Canada Evidence Act*, . . . the Crown through Mr. Thompson [the foundation witness] has failed to establish a proper foundation. As I have stated, he can provide the court with no assistance with respect to where the documents came from, how they were prepared, where the information came from that is set out in them, the billing procedures of the telephone company, and so on.[38]

Therefore, while there is no express requirement given in section 30 that the maker of the record must be called to testify, to ensure admission of electronic evidence under the *Canada Evidence Act*, or under the common law business records exceptions to the hearsay rule, foundation evidence should be provided to demonstrate the reliability and trustworthiness of the record keeping system.

(B) Provincial

The Evidence Acts of British Columbia, Manitoba, Ontario and Saskatchewan contain comparable definitions of "business" and "record", and provide for similar exceptions to the hearsay rule for business records.[39]

Section 35(2) of the *Evidence Act* (Ontario)[40] governs the admission of business records and provides:

> Any writing or record made of any act, transaction, occurrence or event is admissible as evidence of such act, transaction, occurrence or event if made in the usual and ordinary course of any business and if it was in the usual and ordinary course of such business to make such writing or record at the time of such act, transaction, occurrence or event or within a reasonable time thereafter.[41]

Subsection 35(4) provides:

---

38 *Infra*, at 416.
39 *British Columbia Evidence Act*, s. 48; *Manitoba Evidence Act*, s. 49; *Ontario Evidence Act*, s. 35; *Saskatchewan Evidence Act*, s. 31.
40 R.S.O. 1990, c. E-23.
41 *Ibid.*

(4) The circumstances of the making of such a writing or record, including lack of personal knowledge by the maker, may be shown to affect its weight, but such circumstances do not affect its admissibility.

(C) *United States*

The business records exception is codified in the *Federal Rules of Evidence* 803(6) and permits the admission of:

a memorandum, report, record, or data compilation, in any form, of acts, events, conditions, opinions, or diagnoses, made at or near the time by, or from information transmitted by, a person with knowledge, if kept in the course of a regularly conducted business activity, and if it was the regular practice of that business activity to make the memorandum, report, record, or data compilation, all as shown by the testimony of the custodian or other qualified witness, unless the source of the information or the method or circumstances of preparation indicate lack of trustworthiness.

The elements of this exception are:

- the record must have been made in the course of a regularly conducted business activity;
- the record must have been made by a person with knowledge of the information contained in it; and
- the record must have been made at or near the time the information was obtained.

The *Federal Rules of Evidence* 803(6) have been used to admit the following types of records:

- computer-generated telephone toll logs;[42]
- summary of ATM transactions;[43]
- computer records recording entry times of vehicles into the United States;[44]
- payroll computer records;[45]

---

42 *U.S. v. Linn*, 880 F.2d 209 (9th Cir. (Wash.), 1989).

43 *U.S. v. Bonallo*, 858 F.2d 1427 (9th Cir. (Or.), 1988).

44 *U.S. v. Puente*, 826 F.2d 1415 (5th Cir. (Tex.), 1987).

45 *U.S. v. Croft*, 750 F.2d 1354 (7th Cir. (Wis.), 1984). Admitted routinely made and recorded laboratory analysis of drugs as business records under the *Federal Business Records Act*, 28 U.S.C. section 1732. At 1364, the Court stated

It is well-settled that computer data compilations may constitute business records for purposes of *Fed. R. Evid.* 803(6) and may be admitted at trial if a proper foundation is established.

- computer printout generated by keypunch operator as transcribed from another source;[46] and
- computer printout of drug analysis.[47]

(c) Exceptions—Admission of a Party/Declarations Against Interest

Where the computer-produced evidence was produced by the opposing party, it may be admitted as an admission of that party.[48] Admissions are statements made by a party to the litigation (including an accused in criminal proceedings) prior to trial, in which the party admits to facts which help to refute that party's claim or defense, or which assist in the proof of the opposing party's claim or defense. A presumption of reliability is applied to admissions, because rational individuals will not admit to facts that detract from their legal position or that may expose them to liability unless such facts are true. The fact that legal proceedings are contemplated or actually in process can provide additional support to the reliability of an admission. Admissions may include evidence in electronic form, or computer printouts of such evidence, produced by the opposing party during pre-trial discovery.

A related exception may also exist for statements made by a non-party where such statements are against the interest of the maker. To be considered a declaration against interest, the statement must have been made in circumstances where the maker would be exposing himself or herself to financial liability or criminal prosecution with some reasonable likelihood. However, this exception will not include statements made in circumstances where the maker believes or expects that the statement will not or cannot be used against him or her.

(d) Where Rule Not Applicable—Admission as Real Evidence

Certain types of computer-produced evidence may be admissible as real evidence. This may be the case where the evidence is being introduced for a purpose other than to prove the truth of a matter asserted (for instance, evidence of a message that is introduced to show that someone had notice of the message, rather than for the truth of its contents). Computer-produced evidence may also be admissible as real

---

46 *U.S. v. Sanders*, 79 F.2d 195 (5th Cir., 1984).
47 *U.S. v. Scholle*, 553 F.2d 1109 (8th Cir. (Minn.), 1977), certiorari denied by *Scholle v. U.S.*, 434 U.S. 940 (U.S. Minn., 1977).
48 MacKinnon, *supra*, at 18 (Canada) and 49 (United States).

evidence where the computer was used as a calculating device, or to record information, automatically and without human intervention.[49]

Hearsay invariably relates to information that has passed through a human mind. Where information is recorded by mechanical means without the intervention of a human mind, the record made by the machine is admissible in evidence provided, of course, it is accepted that the machine is reliable.[50] In cases where a computer has been used to record data, and there has not been any human intervention to affect the accuracy of the computer printout, this information may be admissible to prove the truth of the contents. The computer printout in such an instance would be offered as proof in the same way as films and tape recordings are offered into evidence.[51]

In some circumstances where computer-produced evidence is sought to be introduced as real evidence, courts can take judicial notice of the underlying scientific principle on which a computer (which includes electronic equipment) operates or rebuttable assumptions as to the reliability of the system.[52] For instance, in *R. v.*

---

49 For examples of such treatment by courts in the United Kingdom, see *R. v. Wood* (1983), 76 Cr. App. R. 23 (Eng. C.A.) (printout of chemical analysis treated as real evidence); *R. v. Shephard*, [1993] A.C. 380, [1993] 1 All E.R. 225, [1993] 2 W.L.R. 103, 96 Cr. App. R. 345, 157 J.P. 145, [1993] Crim. L.R. 295 (Eng. H.L.) (held that to the extent that a computer is merely used to perform functions of calculations, no question of hearsay is involved); *R. v. Spilby, supra,* at note 9 (held that information recorded on a computer, without that information having passed through a human mind, amounted to real evidence. However, the court acknowledged that the situation would have been quite different if the telephone operator in the hotel had herself gathered the information, typed it into a computer system and then a printout from such a system was introduced into evidence). See also, *Castle v. Cross,* [1985] 1 All E.R. 87 (admitted printout of an automatic breath testing device in relation to a road traffic offence involving alcohol in the bloodstream of a driver); *Sapporo Maru v. Statue of Liberty,* [1968] 2 All E.R. 195, [1968] 1 W.L.R. 739 (results of mechanical and electrical devices which are achieved without human intervention are admissible in evidence as real evidence).

50 Professor J.C. Smith, "The Admissibility of Statements by Computers", [1981] Crim. L.R. 387, approved by the Court of Appeal in *R. v. Minors, supra,* at note 4.

51 Of course, the reliability of a photographic image sought to be introduced into evidence (such as that from a photo radar device) may still need to be established by means of a certificate, in a prescribed form, in order to provide the circumstantial guarantee of trustworthiness which would allow the admission of the evidence, absent a statement or certification that it is an original photograph or reproduction thereof. See *R. v. Browning,* [1998] B.C.J. No. 2202 (B.C. Prov. Ct.).

52 Judicial notice has been taken in admitting as evidence the readings of instruments such as thermometers, breathalysers, clocks and speedometers. See discussion in R. MacKinnon, *supra,* at note 30; *Gorman v. Brice* (1902), 18 T.L.R. 424; *Peterson v. Holmes,* [1927] S.A.S.R. 419; *Thompson v. Kovacs* [1959] V.R. 229. Once courts have become comfortable with the results of a particular type of scientific device, judges are more likely to take judicial notice of the underlying scientific principles applicable to the operation of the device. In such cases, the required foundation evidence will likely focus

Caughlin,[53] Mr. Justice Godfrey, took judicial notice of the basic workings of video cameras and VCRs. In reaching his decision, he stated:[54]

> Defense has argued vigorously that this [admission of the tapes into evidence] was an error in the absence of 'expert' evidence. I do not agree. While it would have been open to the Crown to have had the equipment and film examined by an expert in the field who could have given opinion evidence as to lack of tampering, etc., I do not see this as a condition precedent to admissibility. The issue is reliability, in the same way that voluntariness is the issue surrounding the confession of an accused. The evidence required to satisfy the trial judge as to the reliability of any given video tape is going to vary from case to case and may, not must, require opinion evidence.

Alternatively, the courts may apply certain presumptions to ease the burden of proof. For instance, in the absence of evidence to the contrary, some courts have applied a presumption that a computer or mechanical instrument is reliable and was working properly.[55] In *Castle v. Cross*,[56] the court was referred to a passage in Cross on Evidence (1979) at page 47 headed "Mechanical Instruments" which sets out a presumption that:

> In the absence of evidence to the contrary, the courts will presume that stopwatches and speedometers and traffic lights were in order at the material time; but the instrument must be one of a kind as to which it is common knowledge that they are more often than not in working order.

The view of the court in *Castle v. Cross* was that "[I]n the absence of evidence to the contrary, the courts will presume that mechanical instruments were in order at the material time."[57]

---

more on the reliability of the particular device.

53 (1987), 40 C.C.C. (3d) 247 (B.C. Co. Ct.).

54 *Ibid.*, at 252.

55 See *Mobil Oil Corp. v. Registrar of Trade Marks*, [1984] V.R. 25 (S.C.); *R v. Spilby, supra*; An evidentiary presumption of reliability may be justified in the case of commercial off-the-shelf software and/or standard equipment. It would be more difficult to justify in the case of custom software or non-standard equipment.

56 *Supra*, at note 49, cited in *Spilby, supra*.

57 It should, however, be noted that in a later case which referred to this decision, *R. v. Shephard*, the House of Lords remarked that the decision in *Spilby* could be supported by the evidence of the sub-manager, who had testified in respect of the operation of the equipment in question, but that it could not have been supported if it had been based entirely on the presumption that a machine was working correctly in the absence of evidence to the contrary.

Some commentators have suggested that a rebuttable presumption is the better way to admit computer-produced evidence, since it eases the evidentiary burden of proof without cutting off the ability of a party to challenge facts accepted by judicial notice.[58] In the absence of the taking of judicial notice or the use of presumptions, foundation evidence will be required in respect of any underlying scientific principle or assumptions as to the reliability of the computer or other equipment.

9.4 THE BEST EVIDENCE RULE

The best evidence rule (also known as the rule against secondary evidence) requires that a party adduce the best evidence available, which in respect of documentary evidence, means that the original of a writing be offered into evidence. Accuracy is the rationale for excluding such secondary evidence as copies or oral testimony relaying the contents of the original document. Copies may contain errors, and oral testimony may be inaccurate. The rule developed at a time when the only way to make copies of an original was by hand, so there was always a potential for human error in making the copies.

A strict application of this rule would make it impossible to prove many facts in issue. The common law therefore developed a number of exceptions to the best evidence rule, based on the same criteria as the exceptions to the hearsay rule, necessity and reliability. Admission of secondary evidence has been found to be necessary where the original is lost or destroyed, in the control of an opponent who refuses to produce it, in the control of a third party who cannot be compelled to produce it, by its nature (*e.g.*, a tombstone) something which cannot be practically or legally brought into court, or a public document which cannot be produced without inconveniencing the public.[59] In order for secondary evidence to be found to be "reliable", it must be "legitimate and trustworthy evidence, inferior to primary solely in respect of its derivative character, and must not consist of conjectural or illegal matters."[60]

The best evidence rule has diminished in importance today, not surprisingly, since copies can now be made accurately and inexpensively, through electronic means such as photocopiers. These generally remove any potential for error or inaccuracy in the copy. In the case of digital works (such as data in a computer system or stored on computer-readable media), the copies can be an exact duplicate of the original.

When attempting to introduce electronic evidence at trial, the best evidence rule may require a determination of whether a computer printout is an "original" or a

---

58 See R. MacKinnon, *supra*, at 21.
59 See E. Tollefson, "Computer-Produced Evidence in Proceedings within Federal Jurisdiction", *Uniform Law Conference of Canada* (1995).
60 *Bramble v. Moss*, L.R. 3 C.P. 458.

"copy".[61] This distinction is perhaps a bit more tricky for the purposes of the common law best evidence rule, as the rule measures the admissibility of the secondary evidence, or copies, against the "original document", rather than just a "record made in the usual and ordinary course of business" (the standard used for the purposes of the *Canada Evidence Act*). As stated by one writer:

> This emphasis on the point of origin may result in printouts always having to be treated as copies, because a printout is not the point of origin: behind the printout is a man-made device from which the printout's message and format originates, and which can reproduce other printouts just like the first, when and as often as the device is directed so to do. It would seem to follow that if the printout is a copy, then the computer's memory, as the point of origin of the message, must contain the original.[62]

In the case of computer-produced evidence, it is not always clear what is an "original" and what is a "copy". When information is first entered into a computer system, it is commonly stored in the system's core memory (for instance, read/write or RAM memory on a PC, which generally has the quickest access time). It is then usually quickly copied to a semi-permanent storage device such as a hard disk so that the system's core memory can be freed up for other tasks. At some point it may also be copied or moved to a magnetic tape or optical disk storage media for longer term storage. The information, as stored in any of the foregoing digital storage mediums, is not perceivable by humans and must be printed out in hardcopy form, or displayed on a computer monitor. Courts have not always been consistent as to when a record stops being an "original" and becomes a "copy" during this process.[63]

In *R. v. McMullen, supra*, the Court emphasized the authentication issue rather than the question of what was an "original" or "copy", which has less relevance in the case of computer records. In *R. v. Bell* the printout itself was held to be the "record". In some cases, the distinction is relevant because if the printout is a "record", its proponent may need to only prove it was made in the usual and ordinary course of business, whereas if it is a "copy" foundation evidence may be required.[64]

In the United States, computer printouts are considered originals under the *Federal Rules of Evidence* (see Rule 1001(3)) and a majority of states have enacted codified

---

61 In civil cases, agreement is often reached between counsel on this issue.

62 Tollefson, *supra*, at note 59.

63 However, with respect to the bank records exception under the *Canada Evidence Act*, computer printouts have been treated as original records. See *R. v. Bell, supra*, at note 26; *R. v. McMullen, supra*, at note 25; *Canada Evidence Act*, section 29(1). See also H. Stewart, *supra*, at note 22, where the author cites a number of cases where courts have tried to fit computer-generated documents into the language of the *Canada Evidence Act*, but without detailed discussion and without any question of the reliability of the system that produced the record.

64 For instance, see section 30 of the *Canada Evidence Act*.

rules of evidence based on the federal rules.[65] Under Rule 1003, a duplicate is generally admissible to the same extent as an original unless:

1.   a genuine question is raised as to the authenticity of the original; or
2.   under the circumstances, it would be unfair to admit the duplicate in lieu of the original.

It is submitted that the concept of an "original document" should have less significance in the case of computer-based evidence. The emphasis should instead be placed on the overall security and reliability of the relevant computer system.[66]

(a) Canada Evidence Act

Subsection 30(3) of the *Canada Evidence Act* provides an exception to the best evidence rule, by expressly stating that *copies* of business records are to be admitted as evidence where it is "not possible or reasonably practicable" to produce the original record. For the *Canada Evidence Act*, determining whether the document is an "original" or a "copy" will determine the level of preparation necessary to seek admission. Where a computer printout that is admitted into evidence is held to be an original record made in the usual and ordinary course of business, the party tendering the document need not present anything in addition to it. However, where the exact same printout is held to be a copy, it must be accompanied by two affidavits—one explaining why the original record is not available, and the second attesting to the authenticity of the copy.

The definition of "business" given in subsection 30(12) of the *Canada Evidence Act* is broad and should generally not pose any problems. It must, however, be borne in mind that this is an exception for "business" records, and not for "personal electronic records".

The definition of "record" given in subsection 30(12) of the *Canada Evidence Act* would also not seem to be a problem, and appears to cover many types of computer-generated records. However, the question of whether a computer record constitutes a "record" has been complicated by judicial consideration.

In *R. v. McMullen*[67] the Ontario Court of Appeal considered the question of whether a computer printout of entries stored in a bank's computer fell within the meaning of a "copy of any entry in any book or record" for the purposes of section 29 of the

---

65   Under Rule 1001(3), an "original" of a writing or recording is the writing or recording itself or any counterpart intended to have the same effect by a person executing it or issuing it . . . If data are stored in a computer or similar device, any printout or other output readable by sight, shown to reflect the data accurately, is an "original".

66   H. Stewart, *supra*, at note 22.

67   *Supra*, at note 25.

Canada Evidence Act. Section 29 provides a statutory exemption from the hearsay rule and best evidence rule for documents kept by financial institutions.[68] The court held that computer printouts were "copies" of any "entries" in "books or records" for the purposes of section 29, and that the information stored in the computer was the "record".

In a subsequent decision, the Ontario Court of Appeal, in *R. v. Bell*[69] held that computer printouts were not merely "copies", but were in fact "original records". The items in issue were copies of monthly statements of the accused's bank accounts, produced by computers. The records were kept by the bank on its computers until the end of the month, when two copies of a statement of account would be printed. One would be sent to the customer and the other would be sent to the branch, where it would be stored for 15 years. The problem in this case was that the bank computers retained no memory of the transactions recorded in the monthly statement after printing; they only retained the final balance in memory. The trial judge had refused to admit these monthly statements in evidence. If *R. v. McMullen* were strictly followed on these facts, the result would be absurd—how can the printout be only a copy, when there is no record retained in the computer's memory? If the printout is only a copy, then what is the record?

The court in *R. v. Bell* resolved this conundrum by refining or restating the decision in *R. v. McMullen*, holding that:

> *McMullen* is authority for the proposition that information stored in a computer is *capable* of being a "record kept in a financial institution", and that the computer print-out is *capable* of being a copy of that record, notwithstanding its change in form. It is not authority for the proposition that the stored information is the only record, or that a computer print-out is only a copy of that record.[70]

In addition, the court in *R. v. Bell* decided that it was possible for more than one record to exist at any point in time:

> It is sufficient to dispose of the present case in respect of the copy of the Royal Bank statement to say that the information in the computer changed its form, and that the bank's copy of the monthly statement then became the "record". It was the only source of reference available to the bank as to the state of the

---

68 Section 29 provides, in part, as follows:
    (1) Subject to this section, a copy of any entry in any book or record kept in any financial institution shall in all legal proceedings be admitted in evidence as proof, in the absence of evidence to the contrary, of the entry and of the matters, transactions and accounts therein recorded.
69 *Supra*, at note 26.
70 *Ibid.*, (1982), 65 C.C.C. (2d) 377 (Ont. C.A.) at 380.

bank account, saving the possibility of compiling a new statement by searching out the original deposit slips, cheques, etc. It was permanent, for it was to be retained by the bank for 15 years. It clearly was a record kept in a financial institution.[71]

It reached this conclusion by finding that it was possible for information to change form:

> Before computers were used by banks, a teller's journal was the original record. The entries in that journal were posted to a ledger, and that became a second record. I have no doubt that the ledgers of all accounts in a branch were collated so as to produce a ledger for the branch, and that became a record. So it makes no difference that the original information changes form, or becomes absorbed in some larger record. The authenticity of the record as evidence is sufficiently guaranteed by compliance with s-s. (2) of s. 29.[72]

The court ruled that it is always a question of fact whether any recorded information is a "record kept in any financial institution", but held that there were a few general propositions:

- a record may be in any, even an illegible, form;
- the form in which information is recorded may change from time to time, and the new form is equally a "record" of that kind of information;
- a record may be a compilation or collation of other records; and
- it must have been produced for the bank's purposes as a reference source, or as part of its internal audit system and, at the relevant time must be kept for that purpose.

A number of other cases have also decided that computer printouts may constitute the "original record".[73] However, the courts are not always consistent in their

---

71 *Ibid.*, at 381.

72 *Ibid.*, at 380.

73 See *R. v. Vanlerberghe* (1976), 6 C.R. (3d) 222 (B.C. C.A.); *R. v. Bicknell* (1988), 41 C.C.C. (3d) 545 (B.C. C.A.), a computer printout of calls to and from a particular telephone generated by an employee of a telephone company, was deemed to be a "record" for the purposes of section 30 of the *Canada Evidence Act*, and not just a "copy" of the record—even though the data remained stored on the actual computer; *R. v. Cordell* (1982), 39 A.R. 281 (Alta. C.A.) decided that a computer printout of a bank statement fell within the meaning of a "record kept in a financial institution" for the purposes of section 29 of the *Canada Evidence Act*. At trial, an assistant manager of the bank was called to testify and produced the computer printout in question. On cross-examination he testified that the print-out was a copy of what remained stored in the computer. The trial judge had refused to admit the printout, but the Court of Appeal overturned this decision; See also *R. v. Shephard, supra,* where the court implicitly accepted that computer printouts of records of telephone calls can constitute the

holdings in this respect. For instance, in *R. v. Hanlon*[74] the court held that a computer printout of certain Department of Fisheries records was a *copy* of an *original* record, not an original record.

Where the information stored in a computer system is itself a copy (that is, the information was copied into the computer from an original document), foundation evidence may be required as to its reliability. In *Markakis v. Minister of National Revenue*[75] the court refused to admit computer printouts of income tax returns into evidence. The original income tax returns had been destroyed. The court held:

> The information used by the Minister for those years was information gleaned from a computer; the computer was purported to contain information identical to that contained in the returns of income. However, there is no proof this is so. The computer operator who transmitted the information from the returns to the computer was not called to testify and it is doubtful whether he or she would have recalled such information in a manner satisfactory to the Court. Neither section 244 of the Act nor any other provision of the Act or other relevant statute I am aware of renders the information contained in the computer print-out of a taxpayer's income tax returns to be proper evidence a Court may accept as *prima facie* evidence of its contents. The information in the computer conceivably may contained errors; it is hearsay. I am therefore of the view that it wold not be possible to find that Mr. Markakis made a misrepresentation in filing his 1974 and 1975 tax returns since these documents are simply not available.[76]

(b) Evidence Act (Ontario)

The *Evidence Act* (Ontario) provides a statutory exception to the hearsay rule and the best evidence rule by providing that the contents of the original document may be proved by proffering a copy of the original.

Proposed amendments to provincial evidence acts (including Ontario's) would replace the search for an "original" record with the need to show the integrity of the record before the court. Integrity is demonstrated by showing the integrity of the record keeping system of which the record is part.[77]

"original record".

74 (1985), 69 N.S.R. (2d) 266 (N.S. Co. Ct.).

75 (1986), 86 D.T.C. 1237 (T.C.C.).

76 *Ibid.*, at 1239.

77 The *Uniform Electronic Evidence Act*; See J.D. Gregory, "Electronic Legal Records: Pretty Good Authentication?", online: <http://www.callacbd.ca/summit/auth-johngregory.html>.

(c) United States

In the United States, some states have passed legislation expressly addressing this issue, granting the human-readable version of data stored on computers, *i.e.,* the printout, the status of an original record. In states that do not have legislation addressing this issue, the common law admits the computer printout as secondary evidence—as the copy. For instance, in *King v. State for Use and Benefit of Murdock Acceptance Corp.*[78] it was held that information stored in the computer constituted the "original", and the printout was the "copy". The "copy" was admissible as secondary evidence as the "original" was unavailable, being in a form which was not readable.

Records stored on electronic media may also be admissible under:

- *Uniform Rules of Evidence*;
- *Uniform Photographic Copies of Business and Public Records as Evidence Act;*[79] and
- *Federal Rules of Evidence* 803(6).

9.5 AUTHENTICATION OF ELECTRONIC EVIDENCE

As previously discussed, an important criteria for admissibility is the requirement of authentication. Authentication is the process by which the authenticity, or genuineness, of a document is established. A document must be authenticated in order to be admissible.[80] If a *copy* or *converted form* of the document is being offered instead of the original, foundation evidence to establish the reliability of any copying or conversion process may also be required.

If admission of the electronic information is sought on the basis of it being real evidence, it will also require authentication. Authentication of real evidence could entail having a witness identify an item, relate it to the issues or establish its condition as the same then and now in relevant aspects. Objections could still be raised if there was an opportunity for contamination or tampering, or if gaps were present in the chain of custody, particularly in a criminal proceeding.[81]

---

78 *Supra,* at note 29. See also *Brown v. J.C. Penney Co., Inc.,* 688 P.2d 811 (Or., 1984).

79 28 U.S.C. Section 1732.

80 See *R. v. Petersen* (1983), 45 N.B.R. (2d) 271 (N.B. C.A.) at 282-85, 294-96; leave to appeal to S.C.C. refused (1983), 46 N.B.R. (2d) 231n (S.C.C.).

81 When evidence is presented to the court, the proponent must be able to show that such evidence is the same thing as that which was seized. One method of doing so is to show the chain of individuals who had possession of the evidence from the time it was seized until it is presented in court, and that it was stored securely during this process.

(a) Potential for Falsification, Fabrication, Tampering and Alteration

Information stored electronically is more vulnerable to accidental or intentional change than information stored in more traditional forms. Some of the risks of change include the following:

- system failures;
- software problems; and
- danger of unauthorized access to the file through other terminals in the network or by hackers.[82]

Another problem with reliance on electronic data is the possibility that these unintentional or unauthorized changes may not be detected. Depending on the complexity and size of the databank, such changes can be very expensive to find, if one is even alerted to the possibility of changes having been effected.

In some cases, electronic evidence may be fabricated. For instance, one computer forensic investigator has described how he was asked by a State Attorney's Office in Florida to review evidence in a child pornography prosecution, and how, after a thorough forensic examination of the defendant's computer, he concluded that the defendant was being framed.[83] In that case, the computer in question was a very old IBM model PS1 computer with a 300 baud modem. A number of inconsistencies were identified:

- The pornographic files found on the computer all had file date/time stamps that were approximately one minute apart. This was not consistent with the time it would have taken such files to be downloaded using the slow speed modem attached to the computer (each would have taken approximately 10 minutes to download).
- The pornographic files were all stored in JPEG format. However, at the time, GIF was the prevailing file format and it would have been unusual to find more than a handful of files stored in the JPEG format. Also, there was no file viewer installed on the computer that would have been able to view JPEG files.
- The graphics capabilities of the computer were so poor that the files were unrecognizable on its monitor.

However, simply because computer-generated records can be altered, they are not "too untrustworthy to be admitted as evidence."[84] An air-tight security system is also not required. In *U.S. v. Glasser*[85] the court stated:

---

82 K. Chasse cited in Tollefson, *supra*, at note 59.

83 D. Douglas Rehman of Rehman Technology Services Inc. See <http://www.sur-veil.com/forensic1.htm>.

84 *U.S. v. Bonallo, supra*, at note 43.

85 773 F.2d 1553 (11th Cir. (Fla.), 1985) at 1559.

The existence of an air-tight security system is not, however, a prerequisite to the admissibility of computer printouts. If such a prerequisite did exist, it would become virtually impossible to admit computer generated records; the party opposing admission would have to show only that a better security system was feasible.

(b) General Methods of Authenticating Evidence

(i) *Admissions*

The Rules of Court/Civil Procedure of most jurisdictions provide for admissions to be obtained with respect to the authenticity of documents.[86] If an admission respecting a document's authenticity is obtained from the opposing party, then no evidence need be called at trial to authenticate the document.

The procedure generally works by one party serving on the other a request to admit, for the purposes of the proceeding only, the truth of a fact or the authenticity of a document. The party on whom a request to admit is served then has a specified number of days after it is served in which to respond otherwise it is deemed to have admitted the truth of the facts or the authenticity of the documents mentioned in the request to admit. A party is generally penalized if it denies or refuses to admit the truth of a fact or the authenticity of a document after receiving a request to admit, and that fact or document is subsequently proved at the hearing.

It is also very common for agreement to be reached between counsel on this issue.

(ii) *Witnesses*

A witness may be called to prove the authenticity of a business record. Authentication evidence may be provided through the identification of the document by the writer or a signatory, or the testimony of a party who is able to identify the handwriting or typeprint. In *Setak Computer Services Corp. Ltd. v. Burroughs Business Machines Ltd.*,[87] the following statement about authentication of business records was made:

> In our Courts, the usual procedure in proving business records is to call a person with personal knowledge of the business of the party producing the

---

86 In Ontario, see Rule 51 of the *Rules of Civil Procedure*; in Alberta, see Rule 190 of the *Alberta Rules of Court*. See also *First National Bank of Oregon v. A.H. Watson Ranching Ltd.* (1984), 34 Alta. L.R. (2d) 110 (Alta. Q.B.) at 131-132.

87 *Setak, supra* at 759.

records and who also has personal knowledge of the circumstances surrounding the preparation of such records.

It may also be possible to authenticate a business record through affidavit evidence without requiring the witness to be present at trial.[88]

At the present time, in many jurisdictions there are no specific statutory rules relating to the authentication of electronic information, like computer printouts. However, authentication of computer-based information, even if produced in readable form through a printout, may require evidence regarding the reliability of the system. In *R. v. McMullen*, the court stated:

> The nature and quality of the evidence put before the Court has to reflect the facts of the complete record-keeping process—in the case of computer records, the procedures and processes relating to the input of entries, storage of information and its retrieval and presentation . . . [89]

On the other hand, in *R. v. Bell*,[90] the court held that where section 29(2) of the *Canada Evidence Act* had been complied with, this was a sufficient guarantee of the document's authenticity, notwithstanding that the document in question was a computer printout.

(c) Establishing the Reliability of Electronic Records

As previously noted, in the absence of the taking of judicial notice, or the use of presumptions, foundation evidence will be required in respect of any underlying scientific principles or assumptions as to the reliability of the computer (including software) or other equipment, and the accuracy of the results produced.

In a civil proceeding, where a party offering the computer-produced evidence is the party that generated and maintained it, the document should not be immune from scrutiny just because it came from a computer.[91] However, a court may be more

---

88 For instance, see Rule 53.02 of the *Rules of Civil Procedure* (Ontario) which provides: "(1) Before or at the trial of an action, the court may make an order allowing the evidence of a witness or proof of a particular fact or document to be given by affidavit, unless an adverse party reasonably requires the attendance of the deponent at trial for cross-examination."

89 *R. v. McMullen* (1979), 47 C.C.C. (2d) 499 (Ont. C.A.) at 507.

90 (1982), 65 C.C.C. (2d) 377 (Ont. C.A.) at 380; affirmed (sub nom. *Bruce v. R.*) [1985] 2 S.C.R. 287 (S.C.C.).

91 H. Stewart, *supra*, at note 22.

receptive to admitting such evidence without the need for substantial foundation evidence where the records had been subject to scrutiny during discovery.[92]

In some cases, courts are having to devise appropriate tests to ensure not only the reliability of the operation of the scientific computing device, but also the accuracy of the scientific principle and assumptions underlying its operation, especially where the evidence is considered "novel scientific evidence" and is produced solely for use at trial.[93] Due to the importance of foundation evidence for the purposes of demonstrating the reliability of computer-produced data, such evidence may be much more complex than that required to prove the reliability of written records.[94]

In the case where a process or system must be authenticated, foundation evidence may need to address:[95]

- the accuracy, completeness and admissibility of the source of the data;
- the reliability of the method used to enter the data into the computer;
- the reliability of the way in which the computer processes the data (reliability of the hardware and software);
- the accuracy of the process used to output the resulting data from the computer; and
- where applicable, the security of the system.

Such testimony may be provided by the "custodian" of the information or other qualified witnesses. The credibility of the process or system may be enhanced if testimony can also be provided regarding periodic reviews and audits of the information contained in the system. A failure to provide proper foundation evidence can result in the court refusing to admit the relevant evidence.[96]

In *R. v. Wood*,[97] the court held that computer printouts would be admissible, as the output of a scientific device, if foundation evidence was available to prove:

- that the computer was correctly operated;
- that the computer was used with the appropriate programs to produce the sorts of results which are under consideration; and
- the calculations performed could be accepted as reliable.[98]

---

92 *Tecoglas Inc. v. Domglas, supra*, at note 2.

93 MacKinnon, *supra*, at 26.

94 *R. v. McMullen, supra*, at note 25.

95 MacKinnon, *supra*, at 43-45.

96 For instance, see *R. v. Rowbotham* (1977), 33 C.C.C. (2d) 411 (Ont. Co. Ct.) where the court refused to admit computer printouts of telephone bills which were not accompanied with evidence to show from where the documents and the data contained in the documents originated, how the documents were prepared and what procedures were followed.

97 *Supra*, at note 49.

98 MacKinnon, *supra*, at 23.

In *U.S. v. Glasser*[99] the court held computer-generated records to be admissible under the following circumstances:

- they must be kept pursuant to some routine procedure designed to assure their accuracy;
- they must be created for motives that would tend to assure accuracy (preparation for litigation, for example, is not such a motive); and
- they must not themselves be mere accumulations of hearsay or uninformed opinion.

In *R. v. McMullen, supra,* the court required the testimony of a bank official in order to admit certain printouts. Such testimony was required to describe the complete system, including the process and procedures relating to data entry, storage, retrieval and presentation of information.

Computer-based records can be altered or forged, as can traditional documents. However, in the case of computer-based records, such forgery or alteration may be more difficult to detect. Some commentators have therefore stressed the need to consider certain factors in proving the integrity of the record keeping or information management process—the party offering the electronic evidence should provide proof:[100]

- of the sources of the data and information recorded in the databases upon which the record is based;
- that the data and information in those databases was recorded in some fashion contemporaneously with, or within a reasonable time after, the events to which such data and information relates;
- that the data and information upon which the record is based is of a type that is regularly supplied to the computer during the regular activities of the organization from which the record comes;
- by certification that use in the court proceedings of the data and information upon which the statements in the record are based does not violate any legal principle of privileged or confidential data and information preventing its disclosure;
- that entries into the databases upon which the record is based were made in the regular course of business;
- that the input procedures in adding to those databases conform to standard practices in the industry involved;
- that one has depended on that same information to run one's business;
- that the computer programs used to produce the printout, reliably and accurately process the data and information in the databases involved;

---

99 773 F.2d 1553 (11th Cir. (Fla.), 1985).
100 K. Chasse, "Computer-Produced Records in Court Proceedings" *Uniform Law Conference of Canada* (June 1994).

- that the records have been kept by a responsible person in charge of alterations to the system; and
- of the security features used to guarantee the integrity of the total information or record keeping system upon which the printout is based.

It may also be easier to prove the reliability of electronic evidence if the following are in place:[101]

- a good description of the information management system (prepared for the purpose of running the system, not for the purpose of contemplated litigation), showing responsibilities, procedures and audit checks and schedules;
- access controls (including firewalls);
- segregation of duties;
- encryption;
- a digital signature, including hashing;[102] and
- public key certificates.[103]

In *R. v. McMullen, supra,* the Ontario Court of Appeal decided that a finding of reliability, based on sufficient foundation evidence, was in effect, a precondition to admissibility of computer evidence:

> I accept that the demonstration of reliability of computer evidence is a more complex process than proving the reliability of written records. I further accept that as a matter of principle a Court should carefully scrutinize the foundation put before it to support a finding of reliability, as a condition of admissibility . . . and that the admission procedures in s. 30 are more fine-tuned than that in s. 29.[104]

However, there have also been cases where the court has accepted the reliability of computer printouts and admitted them (pursuant to section 30 of the *Canada Evidence Act*), without requiring any foundation evidence about the record keeping

---

101 *Ibid.*

102 To create a digital signature of an electronic record, one applies a "hash function" or "digest function" to the record. This mathematical procedure transforms the record into a shorter record (the "message digest" or "checksum") that is unique to the original record. In other words, if one amended the original record in any way and applied the hash function to it, a different message digest would be produced. It is not feasible to figure out the original message from its digest. See J.D. Gregory, *supra,* at note 77.

103 ITSS Legal Issues Working Group, Department of Justice (Canada), "A Survey of Legal Issues Related to the Security of Electronic Information" (7 November 1996). See <http://canada.justice.gc.ca/commerce/toc%5Fen.html>.

104 *McMullen, supra,* at 506.

system.[105] A court may also admit computer printouts "as *prima facie* proof of the matters contained therein" but permit the other party to challenge the accuracy of the record.[106]

It should be noted that in respect of criminal cases, since the standard of proof for evidence tendered by the prosecution is "beyond all reasonable doubt", minor problems affecting the relevant computer equipment may be sufficient to establish reasonable doubt in view of the complexity of many modern computer systems.[107]

(i) *Statutory Requirements Specific to Computer-Produced Evidence: The United Kingdom Experience*

Some jurisdictions, such as the United Kingdom, have passed statutory requirements specific to computer-produced evidence. Different rules regarding admissibility of computer-produced evidence apply, depending on whether the proceeding is a civil or criminal proceeding. With respect to civil proceedings, Section 5 of the *Civil Evidence Act*, 1968 requires that the following conditions be met in order for computer-produced evidence to be admissible:

(i)   the computer was regularly used for activities regularly carried on;
(ii) the computer was regularly supplied with information of the kind in the statement;
(iii) the computer was operating properly or that any defective operation did not affect production or accuracy; and
(iv) the information is derived from that supplied to the computer in the ordinary course of those activities.

With respect to criminal proceedings, the relevant legislation is the *Criminal Evidence Act*, 1965 and the *Police and Criminal Evidence Act*, 1984. Section 69 of the *Police and Criminal Evidence Act* sets out the conditions that must be met for the admissibility of computer-produced evidence.[108] The object of section 69 is to require "anyone who wishes to introduce computer evidence to produce evidence

---

105   In *R. v. Vanlerberghe, supra*, at note 73, Bull J.A. observed: [Section 30] clearly covers mechanical as well as manual bookkeeping records and the keeping of records, and the flow-out or printout of that bookkeeping system clearly falls within the meaning of records in s. 30 and was therefore admissible. . . .

106   *R. v. Sunila* (February 8, 1990) (B.C. Prov. Ct.).

107   For instance, see *McKeown v. DPP*, [1995] Crim. L.R. 69 (Division Court) where printouts from a breath analyzer machine were rejected simply because the machine's clock was inaccurate by 13 minutes.

108   These conditions are distinct from those relating to hearsay, which are set out in section 68.

that will establish that it is safe to rely on the documents produced by the computer."[109]

In *R. v. Minors,* an early case that dealt with section 69, the Court of Appeal observed:

> . . . [C]omputers are not infallible. They do occasionally malfunction. Software systems often have 'bugs'. Unauthorized alteration of information stored on a computer is possible. The phenomenon of a 'virus' attacking computer systems is also well established. Realistically, therefore, computers must be regarded as imperfect devices. The legislature no doubt had in mind such countervailing considerations when it enacted ss 68 and 69 of the *Police and Criminal Evidence Act* 1984.[110]

Section 69 provides:

> In any proceeding, a statement in a document produced by a computer shall not be admissible as evidence of any fact stated therein unless it is shown—(a) that there are no reasonable grounds for believing that the statement is inaccurate because of improper use of the computer; (b) that at all material times the computer was operating properly, or if not, that any respect in which it was not operating properly or was out of operation was not such as to affect the production of the document or the accuracy of its contents;

Paragraph 8(d) of Schedule 3 provides:

> In any proceeding where it is desired to give a statement in evidence in accordance with section 69 above, a certificate . . . (d) purporting to be signed by a person occupying a responsible position in relation to the operation of the computer, . . . shall be evidence of anything stated in it . . .

A number of U.K. cases have considered who would qualify to sign the certificate. In *R. v. Minors, supra,* the Court of Appeal accepted the evidence, in respect of the section 69 requirements, of an individual that had 14 years' relevant experience, and regularly worked with the particular computer at issue, but rejected the evidence of someone who worked in the offices where a different computer was located, and who testified that she had no reason to doubt the reliability of the computer and that she regularly relied on printouts from it.

---

109   *R. v. Golizadeh,* [1995] Crim. L.R. 232 (C.A.), quoting Lord Griffith in *R. v. Shephard,* [1993] A.C. 380 (Eng. H.L.).

110   *R. v. Minors, supra,* at note 4.

In *R. v. Spilby*,[111] the Court of Appeal had to consider a case involving an appeal against conviction of an offense relating to illegal importation of a controlled drug. The evidence against the accused included logs of phone calls made from a hotel, where a co-defendant had been staying, to the appellant's residence and his club from which he conducted some of his business. The appellant argued that printouts produced by a computerized machine, called a "Norex" which was used by the hotel to monitor guests' telephone calls, were improperly admitted as they were not accompanied by evidence from a computer expert knowledgeable about the Norex who confirmed that the machine was operating properly.

Evidence was given by the sub-manager of the hotel that he was familiar with the function of the Norex machine, how it was supposed to work and what is was supposed to do. He gave evidence that at the relevant time the machine was working satisfactorily, that no one complained about their bills, and that if one looked at the information contained on the printouts, they appeared to make sense and were as would be expected. The Court held that the testimony from the sub-manager was sufficient to discharge the burden under section 69 to show that the Norex machine was working properly.

In *R. v. Shephard*,[112] the House of Lords held that it will very rarely be necessary to call an expert to prove the computer is reliable, and that section 69 can be satisfied by the oral evidence of a person familiar with the operation of the computer who can give evidence of its reliability without being a computer expert.

In that case, the accused, when arrested at her home on suspicion of shoplifting, claimed that she had in fact paid for all the goods but had lost the receipt. At trial the principal evidence for the Crown was given by a store detective who stated that she had removed the cash register rolls for the day in question and examined them, but found no evidence of the unique produce codes for the goods found in the accused's car. The issue was again raised as to whether a party seeking to rely on computer evidence could discharge the burden under section 69(1)(b) of the *Police and Criminal Evidence Act* 1984 without calling a computer expert, and if so how. The House of Lords stated that

> Proof that the computer is reliable can be provided in two ways: either by calling oral evidence or by tendering a written certificate . . . It is understandable that if a certificate is to be relied upon it should show on its face that it is signed by a person who from his job description can confidently be expected to be in a position to give reliable evidence about the operation of the computer. This enables the defendant to decide whether to accept the certificate at its face value or to ask the judge to require oral evidence which can be challenged in cross-examination. . . It does not however follow that the

111 91 Cr. App. Rep. 186, [1991] Crim. L.R. 199 (Eng. C.A.).
112 *Supra*, at note 49.

> store detective cannot in fact give evidence that shows she is fully familiar with the operation of the store's computer and can speak to its reliability.

and

> The nature of the evidence to discharge the burden of showing that there has been no improper use of the computer and that it was operating properly will inevitably vary from case to case. The evidence must be tailored to suit the needs of the case. I suspect that it will very rarely be necessary to call an expert and that in the vast majority of the cases it will be possible to discharge the burden by calling a witness who is familiar with the operation of the computer in the sense of knowing what the computer is required to do and who can say that it is doing it properly.

The House of Lords agreed with the Court of Appeal that a store detective was fully qualified to give the evidence, required pursuant to section 69, to show that the cash registers were operating properly, and that in light of her evidence, the cash register rolls were properly admitted as part of the prosecution's case.

9.6 BILL C-54

With respect to Canada, Bill C-54,[113] *Personal Information Protection and Electronic Documents Act*, addresses some of the admissibility issues discussed in this chapter. The Bill contains several provisions which encourage and facilitate the use of electronic media, and address the use of electronic documents as proof, in non-litigation (court) evidentiary matters. Also included are a series of amendments to the *Canada Evidence Act*, which deal directly with the admissibility of electronic evidence. The amendments alleviate the uncertainties surrounding the issue of authentication of electronic documents, and give some guidance on how to go about authenticating such documents.

Section 31.1 sets out that the burden of proving the authenticity of an electronic document lies with the person seeking admission of the document. An electronic document is to be authenticated by evidence capable of supporting a finding that the electronic document is that which it is purported to be.

---

113 An Act to support and promote electronic commerce by protecting personal information that is collected, used or disclosed in certain circumstances, by providing for the use of electronic means to communicate or record information or transactions and by amending the *Canada Evidence Act*, the *Statutory Instruments Act* and the *Statute Revision Act*. The Bill received first reading in the House of Commons on October 1, 1998.

The application of the best evidence rule to electronic documents is clarified in section 31.2 that states that the rule is satisfied:

(a) on proof of the integrity of the electronic documents system by or in which the electronic document was recorded or stored; or

(b) if an evidentiary presumption established under section 31.4 [relating to documents signed with secure electronic signatures] applies.[114]

"Proof of the integrity of the electronic documents systems" is expanded on in section 31.3, which sets out certain examples of how such integrity can be proven. The section provides that the integrity of the system may be proven:

(a) by evidence capable of supporting a finding that at all material times the computer system or other similar device used by the electronic documents system was operating properly or, if it was not, the fact of its not operating properly did not affect the integrity of the electronic document and there are no other reasonable grounds to doubt the integrity of the electronic documents system;

(b) if it is established that the electronic document was recorded or stored by a party who is adverse in interest to the party seeking to introduce it; or

(c) if it is established that the electronic document was recorded or stored in the usual and ordinary course of business by a person who is not a party and who did not record or store it under the control of the party seeking to introduce it.

The problem of computer printouts and the best evidence rule is addressed in subsection 31.2(2). This subsection provides that a printout can satisfy the best evidence rule, irrespective of whether the printout is a "copy" or "original", "if the printout has been manifestly or consistently acted on, relied on or used as a record of the information recorded or stored in the printout."[115]

---

114 Section 31. 4 allows the Governor in Council to make regulations establishing evidentiary presumptions in respect to documents which have been signed with secure electronic signatures.

115 Subsection 31.2(2), Bill C-54.

10

Conclusion

Lawyers and investigators are increasing their knowledge and interest in electronic evidence. This field will likely grow in importance for both civil actions and government investigations. A technical framework for understanding the use of Electronic Media Discovery (EMD) has been provided in this publication. Hopefully, readers have been sensitized to the importance and potential of EMD. The underlying technology is changing quickly and the law is striving to catch up.

This publication has examined the limits of what is technically possible at present with respect to discovery of electronic evidence. It did not, however, answer how far a party must go legally to satisfy its obligations and duties pursuant to the discovery process. Must a party hire a technical expert to assist in the search for electronic evidence? Must deleted documents be resurrected? To what length must a party go to recover deleted documents? How far back must a party review its backup tapes?

The answers to these questions will likely need to wait until the courts or legislatures have had an opportunity to catch up with the new technologies and business practices. The challenge will be striking a fair balance between the need of the party requiring access to relevant information in order to prove its case, versus the burden imposed on the producing party.

11

Appendix

The following is intended to provide an overview of various resources that were available when this publication went to print. The inclusion of a reference to particular vendor or product should not be implied to constitute an endorsement of such vendor or product. The information is subject to change.

11.1 COMPUTER FORENSIC TRAINING COURSES

New Technologies, Inc.
2075 Northeast Division
Gresham, Oregon 97030
Telephone: (503) 666-6599
Fax: (503) 492-8707
www.secure-data.com
www.forensics-int'l.com

New Technologies, Inc. is a developer of forensic software tools used by military agencies, law enforcement agencies, intelligence agencies and major corporations. It also offers a number of training courses including:

- Document Discovery Course (1 Day)—This course is intended to give computer specialists an overview of how electronic documents are discovered and extracted, and to teach lawyers and forensic accountants about the forensic capabilities regarding electronic document discovery and the specifics regarding legal seizure and preservation of such documents.

- Forensic Training Course (1 Day or 3 Days)—This course covers most of the common issues and exposes the participant to forensic techniques and tools. The course deals with security issues as well as evidence issues and is suited for computer security specialists as well as investigators and internal auditors. The same topics are covered in the one-day version with the difference being the inclusion of a hands-on participation component. The topics include:[1]

---

1 For further information see <http://www/secure-data.com/forensic.html>.

- Preservation of Evidence
- Trojan Horse Programs
- File Slack
- Data Hiding Techniques
- Dual Purpose Programs
- Test Search Techniques
- Fuzzy Logic Tools
- Disk Structure
- Data Encryption
- Matching a Diskette to a Computer
- Data Compression
- Erased Files
- Internet Abuse Identification and Detection
- The Boot Process and Memory Resident Programs

Federal Law Enforcement Training Center (FLETC)—A federal training facility that is part of the Financial Fraud Institute of Glynco, Georgia and provides computer crime and evidence courses to prosecutors, law enforcement and military agencies. Course topics include computer seizure, evidence processing, telecom fraud and Internet-related issues.

University of New Haven (West Haven, Conn.)—The university has created a Forensic Technology Institute to provide forensic computer science training.

National White Collar Crime Center (NWCCC)—The NWCCC in Morgantown, West Virginia, has created a Training and Research Institute to address computer evidence training issues for law enforcement agencies.

The Search Group—Based in Sacramento, California, Search offers a wide range of law enforcement training courses, including an advanced Internet investigations course.

International Association of Computer Investigative Specialists (IACIS)—IACIS is a non-profit association that offers computer evidence training to law enforcement computer specialists.

Guidance Software, Inc.
Telephone: (626) 441-3315
Fax: (626) 799-4364
Web: www.Guidancesoftware.com
E-mail: Info@guidancesofttware.com

Guidance Software offers a three-day course on modern *Windows*-based forensic analysis techniques and an introduction to their "case" methodology.

11.2 SOME INTERNET RESOURCES OF INTEREST

- The Cyberlaw Encyclopedia—<http://www.gahtan.com/cyberlaw/>.

- United States Department of Justice—Computer Crime and Intellectual Property Section (CCIPS) at <http://www.usdoj.gov/criminal/cybercrime/index.html>. See the *Federal Guidelines for Searching and Seizing Computers* (July 1994) and the October 1997 Supplement.

- Global Technology Research, Inc.—Computer Crime Investigation Biography at <http://www.aracnet.com/ngtr/archive/investigate.html>.

11.3 COMPUTER FORENSIC CONSULTANTS

The following companies provide various types of computer forensic services:

Berryhill Computer Forensics
P.O. Box 1674
Benicia, CA 94510
Telephone: (888) 745-1405
Telephone: (707) 745-1405
Fax: (707) 745-4100
Web: www.computerforensics.com
E-mail: info@computerforensics.com

Computer Forensics Inc.
501 East Pine Street, Suite 200
Seattle, WA 98122
Telephone: (206) 324-6232
Fax: (206) 322-7318
Web: www.forensics.com
E-mail: cfi@forensics.com

Data Recovery Richmond
1601 Ware Bottoms Spring Road
Chester, VA 23831
Telephone: 1-888-843-9562
Telephone: (804) 768-1055
Web: www.computer-evidence.com

Dockery Associates, L.L.C.
P.O. Box 36384
Indianapolis, IN 46236
Telephone: (317) 823-8939

Fax: (317) 823-2893
Web: www.finder.com
E-mail: dockery@evidence.finder.com

Electronic Evidence Discovery, Inc.
The Financial Center
1215 Fourth Avenue, Suite 1420
Seattle, WA 98161
Telephone: (206) 343-0131
Fax: (206) 343-0172
Web: www.eedinc.com
E-mail: eed@eedinc.com

Electronic Evidence Recovery, Inc.
Suite 427, 1151 Aquidneck Avenue
Middletown, Rhode Island 02842
Telephone: (800) 353-0919
Fax: (401) 635-4465
Web: www.cyberdetective.com
E-mail: tgalligan@cyberdetective.com

Johnson-Laird Inc.
850 NW Summit Avenue
Portland, Oregon 97210
Telephone: (503) 274-0784
Fax: (503) 274-0512
Web: www.jli.com
E-mail: andy@jli.com

New Technologies, Inc.
2075 Northeast Division Street
Gresham, Oregon 97030
Telephone: (503) 661-6912
Web: www.forensics-intl.com
Web: www.secure-data.com
E-mail: info@forensics.intl.com

Ontrack Computer Evidence Services
Telephone: (800) 872-2599
Web: www.ontrack.com
E-mail: sales@ontrack.com

Rehman Technology Services, Inc.
18950 U.S. Highway 441, Suite 201
Mount Dora, Florida 32757
Telephone: (352) 357-0500

Fax: (352) 589-2855
Web: www.surveil.com
E-mail: rtsi@surveil.com

11.4 COMPUTER FORENSIC TOOLS

- *Expert Witness*—This program runs on *Windows* or *Macintosh* computer systems and collects information about the system, its disks and file system without changing data on the computer being analyzed. It will capture all information including that stored in deleted files and unallocated disk space. Unlike an image backup, that must be restored before it can be analyzed, *Expert Witness'* copy is preserved and available for immediate analysis. See <http://www.asrdata.com/ewfaq.html>.

- *SafeBack* (Sydex Corp.)—Bit stream image backup software that has gained wide acceptance by law enforcement and military agencies. *SafeBack* creates mirror image backup files of hard disks. It preserves all data including inactive or "deleted" data. See <http://www.sydex.com/forensic.html>.

- *ViewDisk* (Sydex Corp.)—Finds hidden or deleted data on computer disks. Can analyze a disk for content and consistency, checking for instances where a file extension may not be consistent with the actual file type. Can also be used to search a disk for user-defined words.

- *EnCase* (Guidance Software, Inc.)—Creates an image backup of the target disk, but then permits a review of the hard disk without the need to restore and "run" the backup image. The backup image, that includes all sectors from the target disk (including hidden and unallocated disk space) can be viewed, searched, filtered and sorted without modifying the time stamps on the evidence image. See <http://www.guidancesoftware.com/>.

- *TruErase Utilities* (Electronic Evidence Discovery, Inc.)—Completely removes data associated with a file so that the information cannot be recovered using conventional software and hardware techniques. See <http://www.eed-inc.com/software/index.html>.

- *Data Custodian* (Electronic Evidence Discovery, Inc.)—Image backup software. See <http://www.eedinc-com/software/index.html>.

- *Electronic Document Discovery Suite* (New Technologies, Inc.)—See <http://www.secure-data.com/suite4.html>. Includes a number of programs:

- *CRCMd5* Data Validation Tool—Mathematically creates a unique signature (hash number) for the contents of one or more files, that can be used to identify whether the contents have been altered.

- *DiskSig* Data Validation Tool—Mathematically creates a unique signature of the contents of an entire had disk drive to validate the accuracy of a forensic bit stream image backup of the hard disk.

- *FileList* Evidence Analysis Tool—Used to document the file content of a hard disk and permit timeline analysis of computer usage.

- *Filter-I* Intelligent Filter—Incorporates artificial intelligence fuzzy logic to scan the *Windows* swap file and data remains in file slack and erased file space for fragments of e-mail, word processing or other documents.

- *GetTime* Capture Utility—Used to document the system date and time of a seized computer.

- *IP Filter*—Used in conjunction with *Get Free* and *Get Slack*, that are used to capture data stored in erased file space and file slack, to analyze past Internet activity on a specific computer. Options allow for automatic pattern recognition of e-mail, graphic files and URLs.

- *Seized* Evidence Preservation Tool—Used to limit access to computers that have been seized as evidence. Designed to be placed on a system boot disk to be inserted in the floppy disk drive of the seized computer.

- *TextSearch Plus*—Used to quickly search storage devices for key words or patterns of text. Searches slack and erased space at the same time as active files.

- *Micro-ID* Ownership Branding (New Technologies, Inc.)—Used to mark a computer's hard disk drive with ownership information that can then be read by a corresponding program called *Cop-Only* (available to law enforcement, pawn shops and evidence room managers).

- *Micro-Zap* File Deletion Software (Micro Law Software, Inc.)—This program is used to securely delete a specific file from a disk drive (but does not eliminate data in file slack associated with other files, fragments of data potentially stored in the *Windows* swap file or data stored in erased file space.

- *M-Sweep* (New Technologies, Inc.)—Designed to clean data stored in file slack space, the *Windows* swap file and erased file space. See also *Disk Scrub*. For further information, see <http://www.forensics-intl.com/tools.html>.

11.5 OTHER USEFUL SOFTWARE

- Mahabit's *Autowipe*—Freeware program for Windows that works in the background to monitor file deletions and then automatically rewrites random data to the space that had been occupied by the deleted file. See <http://www.softclub.net/~mahabit/>.

- Jetico's *BCWipe* (Windows 95/98/NT)—Freeware program that adds additional deletion options to *Windows'* Explorer including "delete with wiping" for files and "wipe free space" for drives. Also includes options for wiping of file slacks, wiping on schedule, and wiping of swap file. See <http://www.jetico.com/>.

- ISIS Interactive's *Shiva* (Windows 95/98)—A shareware diskwipe program that also supports wiping of slack space in existing files. See <http://www.isis-software.com/>.

- Webroot's *Window Washer*—Window Washer cleans Netscape & Internet Explorer's cache, cookies, history, the Web site drop down address list, and much more. <http://www.webroot.com/washer.htm>.

- Executive Software International's *Network Undelete* (*Windows* NT)—Shareware program to undelete files that have been deleted in a *Windows* NT system. See http://www.download.com/>.

- Software Shelf International, Inc.'s *Rescue Undelete* (*Windows* NT 3.51)—Recover deleted files from a *Windows* NT system. The program automatically scans the entire volume in seconds, then builds a list of all files that can be restored. The list can be sorted on file name, modified date, size, or condition.

- Wiredred's *Salvage 98 for Netware* (Windows)—Provides an easy to use graphical interface for recovering deleted files from Netware file servers. Deleted files can be searched for by owner, deleting party, or deletion date. Includes flexible filters, bindery and NDS object browsing, and wildcard searching and filtering. See <http://www.wiredred.com/>.

- *Revival* 2.0—Shareware program to recover deleted files. Download from <http://ftp.direct.ca/pub/simtelnet/win95/diskutl/revive20.zip>.

- PGSoft Inc.'s *Save Butt* (*Windows 95/98*)—Keeps track of deleted files to facilitate file recovery.

- LC Technology International, Inc.'s *RecoverNT* (*Windows 95/NT 4.0*)—RecoverNT is an undelete and file-recovery program that can restore files that were not sent to the recycle bin, but were actually deleted. It allows extraction of files from drives with damaged file systems, or where important information has been deleted. It's compatible with all FAT file systems, including FAT32 and NTFS file systems. (See ZDNet's software library at <http://www.zdnet.com/swlib/>).

- *Recover4all* (*Windows 95/98/NT*)—Shareware program to recover deleted files. (See ZDNet's software library at <http://www.zdnet.com/swlib/>).

- Briggs Softworks' *Directory Snoop* (*Windows 95/98*)—Freeware program to recover deleted files. Permits viewing drives at a very low level, the File Allocation Table, raw clusters, and file names of previously erased files. (See ZDNet's software library at <http://www.zdnet.com/swlib/>).

- PowerQuest's *Drive Image Pro*—Creates an exact image of a hard disk (including any deleted by still recoverable data) rather than copying file-by-file. See <http://www.powerquest.com>.

- Symantec's *Norton Utilities for Windows 95—UnErase Wizard*—Recover deleted files.

Index